OPEN ORGANIZATIONS

OPEN ORGANIZATIONS: A MODEL FOR EFFECTIVENESS, RENEWAL, AND INTELLIGENT CHANGE

OSCAR G. MINK
BARBARA P. MINK
ELIZABETH A. DOWNES
KEITH Q. OWEN

Jossey-Bass Publishers • San Francisco

Substantial discounts on bulk quantities of Jossey-Bass books are available to corporations, professional associations, and other organizations. For details and discount information, contact the special sales department at Jossey-Bass Inc., Publishers. (415) 433-1740; Fax (415) 433-0499.

For international orders, please contact your local Paramount Publishing International office.

Manufactured in the United States of America. Nearly all Jossey-Bass books and jackets are printed on recycled paper that contains at least 50 percent recycled waste, including 10 percent postconsumer waste. Many of our materials are also printed with vegetable-based inks; during the printing process these inks emit fewer volatile organic compounds (VOCs) than petroleum-based inks. VOCs contribute to the formation of smog.

Library of Congress Cataloging-in-Publication Data

Open organizations : a model for effectiveness, renewal, and
   intelligent change / Oscar G. Mink . . . [et al.]. — 1st ed.
      p.   cm. — (The Jossey-Bass management series)
   Includes bibliographical references and index.
   ISBN 0-7879-0028-1
   1. Organizational change.   2. Organizational effectiveness.
I. Mink, Oscar G.   II. Series.
HD58.8.O637   1994
658.4'063—dc20   94-22696
                                                                      CIP

FIRST EDITION
HB Printing   10 9 8 7 6 5 4 3 2 1   *Code 94108*

THE JOSSEY-BASS
MANAGEMENT SERIES

CONTENTS

PREFACE

Our Intended Audience

This book is addressed to practitioners — to internal and external professionals in the fields of organization development, human resources, and training as well as to supervisors, managers, and leaders in organizations of all types. In short, this book addresses anyone who might read and apply the material to identify and release an organization's potential more effectively.

The Problem and the Need

People who study organizations in depth will invariably discover that most problems consist of intricate interlocking threads — systems, subsystems, and constraints and feedback, feedforward, and feedthrough loops. This complexity of interactions presents a dynamic puzzle. As organization development consultants, one of our greatest needs — and that of most of our clients — has been to find a way to organize and interpret information to gain a more comprehensive picture of these complex dynamics. Methods of analysis that first study each person in the organization and then examine the organization itself in the context of each person's dynamics proved too limited. We needed an approach that would clarify the relationships between individuals in work groups, between work groups in the organization, and between the organization and its external environment.

To meet this need, we developed the Open Organization Model — the nine-window framework described in this book. The model enables us to study an entire organization, its internal dynamics at various levels, and its relationship to the external environment. It may therefore be effective for both diagnosis and intervention. The model also seeks to overcome two types of narrow thinking that tend to occur in current analysis and practice.

One narrow tendency is the attempt to solve systemic problems by arbitrarily applying specialized techniques independent of the situation. Methods and techniques such as cross-functional task groups, employee involvement programs for continuous improvement, and attitude surveys and conflict resolution seminars can be highly effective when directed at carefully identified organizational needs and definite priorities. But they can also be abused when regarded as magical, packaged answers to organizational ills. Under such circumstances, they may actually worsen the situation by distracting attention and energy from solving crucial problems. What is needed instead is a diagnostic framework that distinguishes between different kinds of problems and their magnitudes at various levels of an organization. The Open Organization Model provides a comprehensive perspective from which to critique, select, and integrate the profusion of management concepts, systems, styles, and improvement techniques that have developed over the years. It offsets the tendency to promote narrow gains through short-term treatments or specialized techniques. It is especially helpful in counteracting "either/or" and fragmented approaches to organizational change.

A second type of narrow thinking is the tendency to regard established structures and processes as inherently opposed to the realization of human values. Much of the literature criticizing bureaucracy (one mode of organization) has rejected nearly all established methods of organizing human effort. Although not the intent of original scholars such as Douglas MacGregor (1960), this view is clearly held by many in humanistic psychology and applied behavioral science, and it seems to permeate numerous organization development endeavors. In our view, established structures and processes are facts of modern life and can be resources for people rather than forces acting against them. The assumption that organization per se is pitted against human potential leads to a blindness to what can be done by and for people through organizations. Given that organizations will probably continue to be a dominant force in the twenty-first century, they need to be more appropriately organized, not less organized. An appropriate framework can propel us toward a synergic relationship between individual human potential and organization potential.

Our Purpose

An effective framework for organization development must provide at least provisional responses to three fundamental questions: (1) What is the healthy state of an organization? (2) What is the current state of this organization? and (3) How can this organization reach that healthy state? If health is defined too narrowly in terms of one condition, such as efficiency, the diagnosis and interventions based upon the definition may have little effect or an entirely different effect than intended. We therefore need a comprehensive theory of the healthy organization — a systematic operational description that accounts for the complexities of people and organizations.

The Open Organization Model is a step in that direction. As a framework for change, the model's value is twofold. First, it presents a valid standard for evaluating the current status of any organization, regardless of its size or purpose. Second, the model pinpoints areas for growth so that a given organization can move toward greater health. The Open Organization Model provides a vision of organization potential, permits systematic diagnosis of organizational growth needs, and allows room for a wide repertoire of methods for releasing that potential.

Through the Open Organization Model, we hope to offer

fresh possibilities for flexibility, creativity, and productivity within an organization. We are not presenting a conclusive theory or a specialized technique. Nor are we prescribing a rigid process to follow. That would be self-defeating and contrary to the very essence of our ideas. What we are presenting is a practical, multidimensional working model that emphasizes organizational openness and continuous improvement. The model has enough innate flexibility that it can be customized to many settings and situations. We have repeatedly tailored it to fit a variety of needs, as have most of our clients. We believe our readers will find the Open Organization Model to be a powerful tool for understanding their environment and explaining the principles of intelligent organizational life.

The Genesis of This Book

The stimulus for the Open Organization Model, originally developed by Oscar Mink and Jim Shultz, came from Gordon Lippitt (1982). Lippitt, who studied with Kurt Lewin (1951), firmly believed that any situation in the life of an organization could be traced throughout the total organization. Our model is based on Lewin's field thinking paradigm, or the notion that everything is related to everything else, and incorporates principles from general systems thinking. By *system,* we mean an abstract model that helps explain some aspect of the world and how things operate. A systemic model considers all components of a system as well as the interplay between those components. From Gareth Morgan's perspective (1986), the open systems view is intuitively simple, for it involves an infinite number of relationships and everything is related to everything else. The interactions of each of its elements can be explored psychologically, sociologically, and culturally. An open systems view thus provides a way to understand and develop organizations so that management processes and individual human energy work together instead of against each other. Our model utilizes unity, internal responsiveness, and external responsiveness — three characteristics observable at any level of an organization. Resource A describes systems thinking in more depth.

The model itself, in a slightly different format, was first described in *Developing and Managing Open Organizations: A Model and Methods for Maximizing Organizational Potential* (Mink, Shultz, and Mink, 1979). The original book was reprinted in 1991 with an epilogue discussing a case study from our work. Although much information from the original book has been retained, the version here is considerably different. The theoretical foundation portion is considerably reduced, and three new case studies are presented and analyzed in depth.

Over the years, the original model has been further developed and refined in our work with business, industry, government agencies, educational institutions, and other organizations. The Open Organization Model originated from the efforts of Jim Shultz, Oscar Mink, and Barbara Mink during the mid-seventies, when our practice included many diagnostic studies of both profit and nonprofit organizations. To work more effectively with these organizations, we needed a comprehensive method for organizing complex data. Oscar Mink's background in engineering and individual psychology, Barbara Mink's strengths in mathematics and learning theory, and Jim Shultz's approach to interdisciplinary thinking in sociology led to the discovery of the dimensions of unity, internal responsiveness, and external responsiveness, which are detailed in Chapter Two.

Our Backgrounds

The authors have been trained in diverse disciplines, yet we have been moving toward some common assumptions about requirements for successful organizational change. As we have worked with organizations, we have struggled with the inability to predict whether or not particular interventions would succeed and to analyze why they did or did not. Before we developed the model, probably as many of our efforts worked as not. We have had subsequent success with at least three out of four efforts at transformation. We attribute our successful efforts to produce change to the nine-window model and its principles, coupled with a truly collaborative transformation plan. With the Open Organization Model, we have been able to identify and produce needed changes on several levels within the organization: in individuals, in and among working groups, and in the whole organization. Application of the model has permitted purposeful, systematic, positive orchestration of our interventions.

Our Conclusions

From these experiences, we have reached several conclusions. First, to implement change successfully, you must work through the existing organizational structure; working around the structure carries a high risk of failure. Second, you must learn to use social influence and power appropriately to achieve the results you want in the organization. Third, you must generate energy for change among members of the organization. Finally, and perhaps most important, you must have a model from which to work, even if it is relatively unsophisticated at the outset. A model helps in determining what data to gather, how to organize the data, and by what criteria to analyze the effectiveness of your actions.

Since we first developed the model, we have worked with almost every type of profit and nonprofit organization, including multinational, high technology, heavy manufacturing, mining, petrochemical, and finance companies; universities; health care, human service, and social welfare agencies; corrections and justice systems; and municipal, state, and federal government agencies, commissions, and task forces. Collectively, we have one hundred years of experience and have served more than three hundred organizations over the past thirty-two years. When we have been able to negotiate clear contracts with clients and reach mutual agreement on appropriate uses and applications of the Open Organization Model, our clients have developed ownership and have achieved consistently good results. The cases discussed in this book illustrate some of these successes. We believe you will be pleased with the results you produce through this model as well.

Overview of Contents

This book is divided into three major parts: Part One, Foundations of Open Organizations, consists of Chapters One through

Three. Chapter One describes the theoretical base of the Open Organization Model and explains how it relates to continuous improvement and learning. Chapter Two discusses the model itself in depth. Chapter Three details the processes with which we apply the model. Part Two, A Guide for Change, consists of Chapters Four through Nine. These chapters illustrate the application of the model by describing and analyzing three case studies drawn from our work: one focusing on the organization level, one focusing on the group, and one focusing on the individual. Two of these cases were successful interventions; one was not. Chapters Four, Six, and Eight introduce each case. Chapters Five, Seven, and Nine analyze our interventions.

Chapter Ten provides a brief summary and is followed by three resources. Resource A presents a basic review of systems theory and relates aspects of it to the Open Organization Model. Resources B and C describe tools and approaches that address various aspects of the model. Resource B focuses on generic tools and approaches; Resource C describes specific resources. These are followed by a reference list and the index. We have not felt constrained to tie each point to formal literature; however, our basic sources are cited in our reference list. In some cases, we have synthesized ideas and techniques from other sources into our own, to the extent that the origins can no longer be identified. In other cases there is no single source.

The following pages describe a compelling approach for viewing organizations and providing leadership for change and transformation in today's global economy. In an environment of constant change and information superhighways, the Open Organization Model can help interpret and clarify the chaos you face.

Acknowledgments

As the authors of this book, we want to recognize the many wonderful people who shaped its creation.

William Hockenberger, of Precision Grinding and Manufacturing, supplied in-depth information from which we wrote the case in Chapters Four and Five. Amy Czapla, Gail Orkin, Daniel Plunkett, and Deborah Vachon, of The Travelers Managed Care and Employee Benefits Operations division prepared case information for Chapters Six and Seven. They helped relay a true story about readily measurable results.

Duane C. Tway, with Consultants in Organization Response and Effectiveness (CORE), made significant contributions about truth and trust. Susan Hareland conducted research and made contributions to the segments about culture and the environment. Tom Shindell conducted research and provided information on action research and action science. Pat Robinson offered materials that helped shape our thinking on values. Ron Mundy of Somerset Consulting Group made significant contributions toward the evolution and refinement of our model, the strategies for its implementation, and the development of software to measure openness.

David Trott and Paul Kavanaugh provided swift and able fact checking and research assistance. Olivia Becerra assisted with permissions and many other supportive efforts. Steve Sheaffer of Somerset Consulting Group also provided valuable research and administrative assistance.

The good people at Jossey-Bass—particularly Cedric Crocker and Pamela Berkman—made this work a reality. Our agent, Ray Bard of Bard Productions, helped see us through some difficult issues. Finally, Lana Castle provided the underlying support system for all the authors. With her efforts, the book became an integrated whole. She is a profound and able human being and a gardener of manuscripts *par excellence.*

Oscar G. Mink   *Austin, Texas*
Barbara P. Mink   *July 1994*
Elizabeth A. Downes
Keith Q. Owen

THE AUTHORS

Oscar G. Mink is professor of adult education and human resource development leadership at the University of Texas, Austin. He received his B.S. degree (1955) in mathematics and secondary education and his M.S. degree (1956) in counseling and guidance from Brigham Young University; his doctorate (1961) is from Cornell University in counseling psychology and family relations (systems). He completed a postdoctoral internship at the National Training Laboratories Applied Behavioral Science Institute, focusing on the behavior of small groups and organizations.

Mink has developed and implemented programs of cultural change and total system renewal, strategic planning, team building, career development, executive leadership development, succession planning, management skills training, organization behavior, and total quality management.

His books include *Statistical Concepts* (1965), coauthored with Amos and Brown; *Developing and Managing Open Organizations: A Model and Methods for Maximizing Organizational Potential* (1979, 1991), coauthored with J. Shultz and B. Mink; *Developing High Performance People: The Art of Coaching* (1993), coauthored with B. Mink and K. Owen; *Groups at Work* (1987), coauthored with B. Mink and K. Owen; and *Change at Work* (1993), coauthored with P. Esterhuysen, B. Mink, and K. Owen.

BARBARA P. MINK is president and a senior consultant with Somerset Consulting Group, a management firm that serves clients in manufacturing, finance, high technology, health care, education, and public service. Mink provides organization development and renewal services to clients in manufacturing, banking, health care, public service, and information systems. Her clients have included the National Assembly of State Arts Agencies; over fifty colleges and universities; Mellon Bank; IBM; Telecom Australia; and Ethicon.

She received her B.S. (1967) and M.A.T. (1968) degrees and her doctorate (1971) from Duke University in mathematics and educational administration. Her postdoctoral work on group and organizational behavior was done at the University of Texas, Austin.

In addition to her work as an organization consultant, Mink is a founding member of the Human and Organization Development Graduate Program of the Fielding Institute, Santa Barbara, California. As such, she directs master's and doctoral level students in the areas of adult learning and motivation, organization theory, management and leadership, and research.

Mink has designed and written workbooks and articles in the areas of organizational transformation, training design, team development, leadership skills, and organizational research. Her books include *Change at Work* (1993), coauthored with O. Mink, P. Esterhuysen, and K. Owen; *Developing and Managing Open Organizations* (1979, 1991); *Groups at Work* (1987) coauthored with O. Mink and K. Owen; and *The Language of Mathematics* (1979).

ELIZABETH A. DOWNES is a private consultant in research, evaluation, and organizational development in Santa Fe, New Mexico. She holds a doctorate (1990) from the Fielding Institute, Santa Barbara, California, in human and organizational systems; a master's degree (1989) from the same institution in organizational development; and a bachelor's degree (1968) in psychology from Newton College of the Sacred Heart, Boston, Massachusetts. Downes has over twenty years of experience working in and consulting to public sector agencies and non-profit organizations. She has consulted in service delivery, system design, policy analysis, social research, unit cost analysis, program and quality evaluation, and managing organizational change. She serves clients in the areas of education, mental health, social welfare, corrections, youth services, substance abuse, and criminal and juvenile justice.

She is actively involved in public policy and strategic planning as the chairperson of the Governor's Juvenile Justice Advisory Committee and as a member of the Mayor's Human Resources Committee in Santa Fe. She has led several highly participatory processes of designing service delivery systems for New Mexico's community-based mental health and youth care. On a national basis, Downes has been instrumental in the design of a federal initiative to assess and recommend system linkages between criminal justice and substance abuse in selected states.

She has taught research methodology and managing organizational change at both undergraduate and graduate levels.

KEITH Q. OWEN is the division chair of social and behavioral sciences at Austin Community College and a senior consultant with Somerset Consulting Group. He has over fifteen years of consulting experience in employee and customer research, diagnosing opportunities for and implementing organizational change, and managing and evaluating the change process. He has worked for a wide range of clients in the health, high technology, manufacturing, oil, and electric power industries.

Owen has developed and implemented programs in customer satisfaction research, data-based strategic planning, participative performance management systems, employee involvement programs, quality improvement teams, and total quality management. In addition, he has coauthored three books and numerous training programs and articles in areas such as change management, high-performance coaching, and leadership development.

Owen received both his B.A. degree (1967) in psychology and physiology and his doctorate degree (1971) in experimental psychology from the University of Texas, Austin. Following his Ph.D. training, Owen completed internships in clinical psychology and organizational development, in which he focused on evaluating the effects of change programs on individual and organizational performance.

OPEN ORGANIZATIONS

PART ONE:
FOUNDATIONS OF
OPEN ORGANIZATIONS

ONE

DEVELOPING OPEN ORGANIZATIONS: CULTURES THAT CAN ADAPT, CHANGE, AND IMPROVE

Our lives today are tremendously complex. We cannot assume that we are dealing with a world of order and certainty or with a predictable work environment. We also cannot achieve organizational stability through standard operating procedures and control that is concentrated at the top. We face rapid technological advances, knowledge explosion, struggles of women and people of color for political and economic enfranchisement, limited raw materials, increasing environmental and social blight, inflation, shifting world politics, and collisions of diverse values and philosophies.

The magnitude and complexity of these changes strain bureaucratic coping mechanisms. The accountability—or even survival—of many organizations has been challenged because of their inability to respond flexibly and appropriately to the needs of their employees, beneficiaries, and environment. A primary task of today's organization is therefore to develop strategies that enable it to identify and cope effectively with significant areas of uncertainty in the environment. Planning must be continuous, and roles and functions must adapt to new conditions as they arise. We are learning to adapt to and transcend the most chaotic events since perhaps the thirteenth century. This chaos exists in all of our major social institutions—economic, military, educational, and religious. These four institutions seek a coordinating institution, one that is served and supported by all the others. Education, or learning, seems to be the current candidate. Technological breakthroughs not only suggest solutions but also produce the majority of the chaos we currently face. The open organization concept provides a way of tapping the collective intelligence of an organization. Our model provides a framework for applying information science and field thinking to create a basis for insight, learning, and problem solving.

Dollars and Diversity

In addition to being aware of the challenges confronting individuals and the organization, contemporary leaders must consider a larger context—the global marketplace. According to the *U.S. Bureau of the Census, Statistical Abstract of the United States: 1993* (Table 660), since 1975, the number of service-related jobs in the United States has been rising steadily, while the number of slightly higher-paying, goods-producing jobs has been steadily decreasing. In 1990, an average retail job paid less than $200 a week (Table 660). In 1991, 14.2 percent of the people in the United States lived below the poverty line ($10,860 for a family of three); over 21 percent of those people were children. Those who work full time on minimum wage make only about $7,600 per year (Famighetti, 1993, p. 135). These events and statistics are part of our larger culture. How do these statistics on wages influence organizations? Low wages keep employees below the poverty line and contribute to their stress. Stressed-out employees tend to be preoccupied by their own problems, and, as a result, cannot make as strong a contribution to their companies and employers.

The *U.S. Bureau of the Census, Statistical Abstract of the United States: 1993* (Table 12) also reveals that the cultural diversity of the United States has changed dramatically. From 1980 to 1990, the U.S. Hispanic population rose about 52 percent and the Asian population rose about 114 percent. The authors consult a great deal in Australia, where there is tremendous cultural diversity. One factory owner with whom we work has five hundred people on his shop floor, and he must deal with over thirty different languages and dialects with those people. We believe that Australia's cultural diversity reflects some of the complexity all nations face or will soon face.

In the United States, the influx of women and people of color into the workforce has brought a wide variety of new expectations, orientations, backgrounds, and communication problems. Some of these problems are primarily identity- or self-oriented. Others are production- and survival-oriented. This diversity of values and motivations has profound implications for planning, development, and operation. The work ethic and profit motive no longer provide cohesiveness and direction for everyone. Quality of life and the challenge and satisfaction of jobs must be considered, along with more diverse values.

The Changing Work Force

One predictable element of the working environment through the late 1950s was a relatively uniform employee value system. The United States had emerged from an agrarian era in which, if you did not work, you did not eat. Workers were willing to subject their identities to the goal of production in return for material survival. However, by the mid-1950s, we had achieved a prosperity that caused some young people to experience another orientation. They said, "First I have got to establish my own identity. Then I will choose my work." Workers from this generation tended to take adequate wages and fringe benefits for granted. They expected jobs to fulfill personal needs, to be interesting, and to propel them toward their objectives (see Herzberg, Mausner, and Snyderman, 1959; Ford, 1969).

However, as we left the postindustrial period and entered the information age, more workers fit Abraham Maslow's description of "self-actualized" people—those uniformly devoted to some task, calling, vocation, or beloved work (1967). They placed meaningful tasks above high wages and satisfying relationships with co-workers above fringe benefits. They placed more value upon certain "being-values," like self-sufficiency (personal mastery), perfection (quality), simplicity, richness, meaningfulness, and *unity* or *wholeness* (see Maslow, 1971). The emphasis on being-values led people to search for more autonomy and responsibility as well as more freedom, creativity, and supportive relationships. A key emphasis of the feminist movement has been its focus on both relationships and achievement. As a result of this emphasis on being-values and relationships, we began to push for (and sometimes achieve) greater equity and more balance in work mores and practices. The shift toward such being-values can occur only in an atmosphere of openness and trust, which leads to several key questions. What kind of an environment enables the pursuit of such being-values? What would an organization that enables people to achieve such values emphasize? We maintain that such an organization would support:

- Truth
- Freedom, self-management, and self-direction
- Empowerment
- Justice
- Meaningful, constructive collaboration

We call such an organization an "open" organization, and we next explore what we mean by openness.

Bureaucratic Versus Open Organizations

Openness can best be understood by contrasting open organizations with bureaucratic organizations. They tend to differ in seven major categories: (1) structure, (2) atmosphere, (3) leadership, (4) planning, (5) motivation, (6) communication, and (7) evaluation. Any organization or system can be described on a continuum from completely closed to completely open — from continuity to change — although no system reaches either extreme. Table 1.1 clarifies these and other aspects of the open organizations concept.

Table 1.1. Closed (Bureaucratic)
Versus Open (Future-Oriented) Organizations.

	Closed, Bureaucratic Organizations	Open, Future-Oriented Organizations
Structure	Pyramid, bureaucratic, hierarchical Rigid, static, ritualistic Rules, laws, procedures	Flexible, temporary (task forces, ad hoc) Holistic, responsive, purposive Networks
Atmosphere	Chain of command Formal, aloof, low trust Competitive/win-lose	People centered, caring Informal, warm, intimate Goal oriented/win-win
Leadership	Controlling, seniority important High task, low relationship Assumes worker immaturity/dependence Values seniority-related experience Low risk	Innovative, creative High task, high relationship Interdependent, mature, teamwork Personnel development, career planning High risk, experimental
Planning	By top management Emphasizes rational, legal mechanisms Policy making and implementation Highly political (territoriality)	Relevant participation by all those affected Collaborative policy making and implementation Decision making by problem solving
Motivation	By external rewards and punishments	Intrinsic, positive expectations Learning contracts
Communication	One way, downward Hidden agendas, repressed feelings	Multichannel (upward, downward, lateral) Feelings expressed (respectfully)
Evaluation	Performance appraisals Subjective Budget referenced (average %) By supervisor	Goal oriented Objective and subjective

Continuity	Change

← ─────────────────────────────────────── →

Source: Adapted from Mink (1986, section 3, p. 6).

Open systems also differ from closed or bureaucratic systems in their approach to problem solving. While bureaucratic organizations often approach problems from a blaming orientation (Who/what caused the problem?), open organizations focus on solutions (What is the existing situation? How would we like things to be? What is the difference?). It is usually best to deal with a problem by focusing on its cause, confronting the problem itself rather than trying to determine who or what is to *blame*. As Peter Senge says in *The Fifth Discipline* (1990, p. 43), "The system's perspective tells us we must look beyond the individual mistakes or bad luck to understand important problems. We must look beyond personalities and events. We must look into the underlying structures which shape our individual actions."

The following characteristics describe ideal open organizations:

- Rather than focusing energy on power issues, open organizations consistently focus on defining and achieving their purposes and goals by creating commitment, attaining alignment, and improving productivity. They share information and act on consensus. Their leaders use a systemwide perspective when solving problems and rely only secondarily on legal or economic coercive authority.
- Open organizations focus on achievement of goals through collaboration and working together rather than through application of authority. This collaboration demands generosity from all who agree to participate.
- Open organizations constantly interchange activities, data, and energy with those upon whom they depend (for example, their customers and suppliers). The organization represents its purpose to outside groups and gathers information that may influence decisions and goals. Open organizations are *proactive* rather than *reactive* in relation to their environments. They can therefore anticipate and prepare for changes rather than make decisions after crises have developed. Learning and continuous improvement become a way of life.

An open organization with full interaction among all its parts and with its environment either already has the resources and energy for change or will acquire what is needed. It will have a clear vision and mission, it will work toward specific short- and long-term goals, and it will tap its leadership and its environment for needed guidance and energy within the framework of its own culture, its customer expectations, and its leadership initiatives.

Adaptability and Paradigm Shifts

According to the open systems view, adaptability encompasses both a capacity for internal responsiveness, external responsiveness, and a support for unity of purpose. Effective planning must account for diverse motivations and values and the perspectives and resources of employees, customers, and vendors. In the bureaucratic hierarchy decisions are made at the top and passed down. The thought given to views and aspirations of personnel at lower levels depends on the wisdom and personalities of the authorities. Often vendors are excluded and customers merely tolerated. The open systems approach, on the other hand, demands that planning be organization-wide and ongoing, with customers and vendors viewed as integral parts of the total enterprise. All constituents provide input and feedback, with the group recognizing the special competencies of individual members and with competence serving as the crucial element in decision making.

To be effective, organizations must learn how to deal with their changing environment and the changing needs of their own people. While some of the dimensions of current and future environments are predictable, many are not even known. Therefore, if organizations are to respond successfully to diversity and change, they need people who can think, learn, and adapt, who are flexible and creative, innovative, and collaborative. They must also help people become more adaptable and better able to deal with the challenges of life.

Swiss psychologist Jean Piaget (1957, 1980) defined intelligence as adaptability and continuous learning. In *Freedom to Learn* (1969, p. 163), Carl Rogers said "the most socially useful learning in the modern world, is the learning of the process of learning . . . a continuing openness to experience and incorporate into oneself the process of change." That idea is at the very heart of continuous improvement and the learning organization. Senge, writing on massive change, notes the "organizations that will truly excel in the future will be organizations that discover how to tap people's commitment and capacity to learn at all levels in the organization" (p. 4). We believe that these same people must also be psychologically healthy so they can be open to new experiences and be aware of the systems — both human and technical — that surround them. They need to find information, relate it to current problems, and solve those problems quickly, time and time again. They will therefore be in a process of continuous learning, adapting, and transforming.

This emphasis may require a new way of thinking, a new mental model, or what some call a "paradigm shift." This book explores the shift from bureaucratic to open organizations and the disciplines required to make that shift. To explain the concept of shifting paradigms, we will use the analogy of *The Wizard of Oz*. This movie begins in black and white, and then transforms into glorious Technicolor when a tornado sets Dorothy's house down in the Land of Oz.

Between Two Paradigms

What happens between Kansas and Oz? A lot of things can happen, for we are dealing with different cultural perspectives. We are exploring the difference between what was and what will be in the future.

Because of the extent of such potential changes, the term *paradigm shift* seems inadequate. We are not merely shifting; we are breaking out of a mold. We are exploring a whole new way of thinking. We are being swept up by the tornado. This change requires constructing new paradigms that will work with new types of organizations, leadership, and atmospheres: these new paradigms will require "transformational leadership," which values innovation and creativity and envisions the future, versus "transactional leadership," quid pro quo, which values and assumes a stable world.

These new paradigms also necessitate that we reconsider the meanings of planning, motivation, and communication in organizations. We must examine the difference between learning and performance. We must change how we evaluate and recognize people. We must consider new reporting relationships. We must develop new attitudes toward customers.

These changes involve more than a single variable. They involve several levels and several dimensions. The new awareness of and valuing of organizations' leaders, employees, vendors, and customers create a complex arena, and we need some kind of template with which to view it—a template that provides a way to examine the interplay of all organizational components to see how they influence each other.

Magic and Vision

But in the business world most managers and practitioners do not want systems and templates; they want magic. "Don't talk about three to five years hence," they say. "We want a one-day communications workshop," or "Let's look at diversity issues. Can you do that in two days?" We need to avoid the mindset of short-term fixes and begin to examine long-term solutions. We must learn to think systematically if we are to cope with massive paradigm "shifts."

Like Dorothy, the Scarecrow, the Tin Man, and the Cowardly Lion, we are already heading down the Yellow Brick Road. We are already in the midst of massive organizational shifts. And we must consciously choose to "follow the yellow brick road." If our organizations are to survive, we have no other choice.

So we need to understand more about change. Change is not simple. It is not just another magic solution. Change begins on a personal level. It occurs first within individuals. These personal changes are in turn reflected in work groups, organizations, and larger human systems. When confronting change, we are concerned about how it will affect us. Those wishing to facilitate change must therefore learn to deal with people's fears and insecurities about change and learn to anticipate, legitimize, and accommodate their concerns. These concerns are inherently neither good nor bad; they are merely developmental stages people go through when confronted by change. But these stages of concern are real and must not be ignored. People must be guided and supported as they work through them; they cannot be forced to drop one unresolved concern and move on to another. And for each new change or innovation, this predictable developmental cycle will be repeated. (For extensive information on stages of concern, see Hall, George, and Rutherford, 1979; Hord, Rutherford, Huling-Austin, and Hall, 1987.)

It is important to understand that, in its operational framework, change is multidimensional and does not happen quickly. While making a change, we need to examine our values. We need to build a different kind of climate, where everything is open to discussion and we can reveal false wizards when the need arises. We need to be aware of the power structure, and work within it and through the normal power channels and existing management structures. Within this context, leaders can generate the energy for change through shared goals, shared values, and shared visions. Progress needs to be monitored continually. Such a change can take place only in an atmosphere of openness and trust. Openness and trust provide the foundation for the collaboration required to enable successful learning and problem solving.

Openness and Trust

Most people will acknowledge the importance of open communications. But in many organizations, information is still used for power and control and is not shared. Most of us have yet to achieve true openness and honesty. A crucial step toward openness is to recognize the need for sharing information openly. Chris Argyris has written extensively about the importance of "informed choice" and "discussability" versus "undiscussability" (1974, 1982, 1985, 1990). Oftentimes a lot of issues need to be discussed, but many of them are still under the table. Managers still hide their dissatisfaction about employees' performances. Leaders still form task groups without providing adequate support. Organizations spend big dollars to reengineer processes on paper and then fail to execute changes in relevant human and technical systems because leadership does not have enough information about the complexities involved and the timelines required for implementation. Typically, they have been ill informed by other employees or by consultants. To learn and grow, people need access to that information. Learning involves searching for different solutions. Learning involves taking personal responsibility for building excellence and highly productive organizations. The degree of openness will allow us either to do more of the same or to change and operate in a different paradigm. Clearly, we are not in Kansas anymore. We are still in the wrath of the tornado. We have not yet reached Oz.

Intelligence, Caring, and Courage

Three resources accompanied Dorothy on her trip down the Yellow Brick Road toward Oz. The Scarecrow had intelligence. The Tin Man had heart. The Cowardly Lion had courage. And when they reached the Wizard, they learned he was only a little person behind a great big screen, using a loudspeaker and lights and smoke. But what he did was to affirm that they already had the characteristics they desired and the power they required to create their own magic. He gave them small tokens that strengthened their belief in themselves.

Helping people discover what they already have — that is how we need to empower the people with whom we work. If we are developing self-managed work teams, if we are implementing multilevel changes, we must assume that people are doing the best they can to make changes happen. To facilitate the process, we must allow them to continue learning. We must structure our programs and our interventions to support people learning, exploring, and innovating.

Those who wish to promote organizational openness must confront their own level of openness, for they cannot model a level of personal being that exceeds their own level of psychological functioning. Yet no manager possesses every potential strength and capability. Like everyone else, managers have their own preferred styles of perceiving and relating. Open systems managers, however, are committed to developing capacities within themselves that they may have previously ignored. Then they may collaborate with others who have complementary strengths and resources.

Changing our values about diversity, true collaboration, innovation, adaptability, and learning is not easy. Dealing with these challenges requires tremendous courage. We must learn to examine our actions — even in the process of acting. We will have to use our hearts, our heads, and our courage to implement a long-term strategy, and we will need good, consistent models that allow for positive changes.

Summary

To function and excel in today's global economy while coping with the challenges of an increasingly diverse work force and constantly changing information and technologies, modern organizations must create new paradigms that focus on adaptability, learning, and openness. These paradigms must allow people to experience, reflect, learn, and grow. Then they must support those who value openness, people, systems, and the organization as a whole. This process requires much intelligence, caring, and courage, as well as an understanding of the many possible interrelationships and the dynamics inherent in any organization. Forward-thinking organizations must acknowledge that human life is organic and fluid rather than mechanistic and that it involves emotions as well as intellect.

The organization of the future will be based on adaptability — intelligence, continuous change, and (when needed) transformation — rather than on predictability. Process will be more important than structure, and free human interaction more effective than impersonal, chain-of-command hierarchy. It will be an intelligent, adaptable organization that can respond to shifts in a changing social environment — an organization in which all human energies are focused toward a common end.

TWO

CREATING UNITY
AND RESPONSIVENESS:
THE OPEN ORGANIZATION MODEL

This chapter describes the heart of the book: the Open Organization Model (or nine-window model). The openness we advocate is quite natural to reasonably healthy human beings, who are centered and organized around a unified value system. Their behavior is congruent with their values. They care for themselves and engage in genuine, caring relationships with others.

In this chapter, we first discuss the three characteristics of openness and the three basic levels of an organization. Then we examine the key qualities that relate to each of the nine windows in the model and clarify our vision of the open organization.

The Open Organization Model

Figure 2.1 is a graphic representation of our model. This framework illustrates the *entire* organization (or system) in its healthiest state and establishes an ideal structure for evaluating relative openness and guiding a given organization to greater effectiveness.

The nine windows of the Open Organization Model provide a way to conceptualize interrelationships in an organization. The model views an individual, a group, or an organization

Figure 2.1. The Open Organization Model.

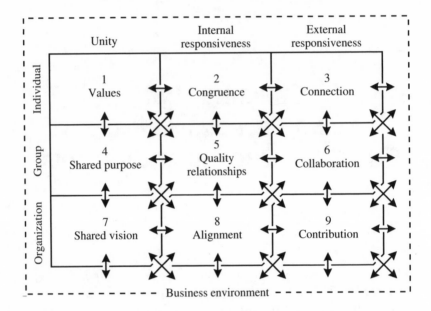

as a system composed of subsystems located within a larger business environment, or system. The dotted line at the edge of the figure represents the overall openness at all levels. The Open Organization Model helps us determine how well these systems are functioning internally, in relation to each other, and in relation to the business environment.

Characteristics of an Open Organization

The Open Organization Model examines three characteristics — unity, internal responsiveness, and external responsiveness — that are present within three basic levels of an organization: the individual, the work group, and the entire organization. (We could also expand the model to encompass further levels — for instance, the community and humanity as a whole.)

Unity. Unity refers to integrated wholeness, coherence, or centeredness. It is the organizing dimension of any biological life or physical form. It guides the growth of an organization into a cohesive whole like the double helix of DNA coding guides the growth of an organism into a functioning life form. Many terms have been used to label unity in a human system: (1) at the individual level — ego, ego states, identity, self, self-concept, perceived self, persona, personality; (2) at the group level — syntality (group personality), purpose, mission; and (3) at the organization level — shared values, vision, mission, and goals. All of these terms describe how individuals, groups, and organizations show consistent, unifying, purposive, and self-organizing behavior in varying environments.

Unity permits and promotes awareness of self, of other components (such as work groups), and of the external world. It is the essence of being and becoming, enabling adaptability or intelligence. In open organizations, unity is maintained and enhanced by consistently focusing energy on the definition and achievement of purposes and goals, rather than on power issues. Organizational purpose is sharpened, modified, and realized through open discourse that takes a constructivist position of confrontation, shared information, transformational learning, and consensus-creating activities (Mezirow, 1991). These activities reflect internal responsiveness.

Internal Responsiveness. Internal responsiveness refers to the ability of component parts to align and work together toward a common purpose. In an open system all parts respond to each other rather than being fragmented, rigid "empires." All parts of an open system are themselves open systems. For example, the organs of the human body are open, interdependent subsystems that exchange nutrients, oxygen, nitrogen, and other elements of biological functioning that create life energy. When the free exchange and flow of life elements is blocked, disease results. Human organizations also develop blocks, with closed, belligerent members or defensive departments.

In an open organization, internal responsiveness is developed and maintained through collaboration rather than through authority. Through collaboration, people focus on achieving accepted goals and work together to plan and implement their shared vision. Such collaboration involves generosity and sacrifice. This process assumes that, given opportunities to develop, people have the capacity for creativity, responsibility, and self-organizing growth experiences.

External Responsiveness. An organization does not become unified or centered by isolating itself from the outside. Unlike the fanatic who becomes secure in a closed, oversimplified worldview, the open organization is unafraid of new data. In an externally responsive organization, information flows readily in and out of the organization so its products, services, and systems can adapt readily to changes in its social, economic, and technical environment. This interchange is a continual series of planned transactions through which the organization represents its purposes and needs to outside groups and gathers information and support that may affect its decisions and goals.

An open system has the processes and skills to assimilate new data into planning and setting goals. It is proactive or transformative rather than reactive in relation to the external environment. An open system anticipates and prepares for changes, making decisions before crises have developed. It can therefore maintain unity while remaining both internally and externally open.

External responsiveness in an organization comes from the continuous interchange of activities, data, and energy with the other systems it serves or depends upon. Such interchange requires permeable system boundaries.

Organizational Boundaries

Each part of the open organization is separated from the others by invisible, permeable, shifting boundaries that take many forms, share different relationships, and operate with varying governing rules and functions. Windows or systems can be either open or closed, meaning that their boundaries are either responsive (open, permeable) or unresponsive (closed, not permeable) to receiving input or giving output to the other parts.

The Open Organization Model views the organization as an energy exchange system that continually shares activities, information, and energy with other systems in the environment. In chaotic environments, information determines the form an organization takes. This energy interchange is an ongoing series of transactions—both planned and unplanned—in which the organization gathers information that may affect decisions and goals and represents its purposes to outside groups, and vice versa. The two-way arrows in Figure 2.1 illustrate the interdependence and interchange among individuals and groups, individuals and the organization, groups and groups, and groups and the organization.

An open organization, by design, has open (or permeable) boundaries—both between the organization and its environment and between individual components within the organization. This openness is prerequisite to the organization's ability to provide quick, relevant responses and to adapt to a rapidly changing business environment. These responses may be routine, may engage others in collaborative problem solving and renewal, and often lead to transformative processes and metalearning (learning how to learn).

Levels of an Organization

The characteristics of unity and internal and external responsiveness may be observed at three levels: individual, group, and organization.

Individual Level. At the individual level, unity relates to self-concept ("I know who I am, and I appreciate my uniqueness") and to self-worth and self-esteem. Internal responsiveness involves an awareness of one's wants and needs and the permission and action to fulfill them. External responsiveness refers to interacting with others to produce mutually beneficial results—reaching out, listening, responding, being open, and searching for new frames of reference, new premises, and transforming experiences.

When applied to customer service, self or unity statements would include "I value this customer," "I appreciate the importance of customer service," and "I will serve our customers to the best of my abilities." An internally responsive statement might be "I want to do a good job with this customer." An externally responsive statement might be "Please tell me how you like our service and what I can do to improve."

At this level, we work with individuals' value sets and invite concerned participants in the change effort to examine self-awareness, internal responsiveness, and quality interpersonal relationships. Action science and critical reflection become critical for transformative learning experiences. (Chapter Three discusses these processes in more detail.)

Group, or Team, Level. Group unity involves commitment to group purposes, goals, and tasks. Unified group members move collaboratively in the same direction. Internally responsive group members are aware of one another and are sensitive to others' wants and needs. They support one another, provide useful feedback, and develop and maintain good relationships. Each person is accountable for his or her own behavior. Group external responsiveness refers to cooperative interaction with other groups or components within the organization. Externally responsive groups link well with other groups and gather information from them for group problem solving. Responsive groups provide top-quality products and services to both internal and external customers. Such groups learn together and constantly improve. They optimize problem solving by utilizing a more complete, shared information base and, when required, transform relationships by participating in problem-setting and problem-reframing processes.

Organization Level. At the organization level, unity involves rallying around a purpose—vision, mission, key goals—aligning values, and clarifying the organization's strategic needs. Internal responsiveness refers to the interactions among different components within the organization. Departments must openly share information, exchange quality products and services, and cooperate and collaborate rather than compete with each other. External responsiveness at the organization level involves how the organization interacts with the community. Externally responsive organizations gather information from customers, vendors, and other stakeholders when planning and setting goals. They offer relevant services to constituent groups. They do what is needed to provide customers with quality products and services. The bottom line for the entire system is satisfied, excited customers who are served by employees who are valued and well treated by their organization.

Unity and internal and external responsiveness are normal states for healthy systems, both small (a cell, a person) and large (a group, organization, or society). These characteristics are inherently interrelated, and different organizations reflect each characteristic on a continuum between extremely open and extremely closed.

Table 2.1 summarizes the behaviors and characteristics that maintain and enhance openness at each level of an organization.

Qualities of an Open Organization

The key words in each of the nine windows shown in Figure 2.1 represent nine basic qualities found in open organizations. These qualities tend to develop progressively and depend highly on one another. A wealth of information is available on each quality, so here we offer only a brief discussion of each window. Many other descriptors could be used for these windows, and we encourage readers to tailor the model to meet their specific needs. Here we have chosen those words that communicate the essence of each window in the most situations.

Window One: Values. The very cornerstone of an open organization is values at the individual level (window number one). Values are beliefs based upon our most fundamental understanding of our world. They form the basis of self-concept or self-image. They provide a context for decision making and action taking, thereby enhancing a person's capacity to self-organize. Our personal focus at any one moment typically reflects the value

Table 2.1. Open Organization Behaviors and Operations.

	Unity	Internal Responsiveness	External Responsiveness
Individual	• Identification of my basic beliefs, who I am, my uniqueness, self-concept, perceived self • Values—open and other-oriented as opposed to closed and self-oriented	• Awareness of myself, my feelings, my needs, my defenses • Freedom to fulfill my wants and needs • Personal congruence • Critical reflection on premises, frames of reference, and attributions about self and others	• Hearing and responding to others; active, constructive listening • Openness to ideas, experiences, people • Love—ability to enter into and establish enduring relationships • Interpersonal attraction and involvement
Group	• Identification of team purpose, goals, and objectives; team building • Shared values • Achievement of syntality (group personality) and synergy (group output greater than the sum of individual outputs)	• Interpersonal skills • Facilitation of interaction among team members • Process observation • Sensitivity and coherence • Interpersonal attraction or cohesiveness	• Gathering and relating external information relevant to team tasks • Linkage with other individuals and groups • Cooperation with other systems to achieve a common purpose
Organization	• Development of common goals of organization • Leadership according to purpose, vision, and mission • Shared values	• Responsiveness between components within the organization • Data sharing • Organization development and human relations • Links between individuals and groups	• Responsive to larger community • Social relevance • Profitability • Meet or exceed customer expectations • Work closely with vendors as partners

Source: Mink, Shultz, and Mink, 1979/1991, p. 14.

base around which the "self" is organized. This value base provides the context from which we perceive what is important and worth living for, what is real, and what is possible. Like any framework, it can be life enhancing or life destroying. The framework itself is neither intrinsically good nor bad; it can be judged only by the outcomes of the choices that flow from it. The framework of the Open Organization Model is based on the values of love, justice, truth, and learning.

Open systems enhance individual feelings of worthiness and trust in the intrinsic goodness of others. They encourage the acceptance of individual differences and the honest expression of feelings, even when those feelings are confrontational. Such openness requires a climate of two-way communication between all components of the system, whether internal or external.

At their inception, organizations usually expend considerable attention and energy on clarifying their purpose and underlying values and on integrating organizational values with those of individual members. In fact, people who start enterprises often do so because of their shared values. Eventually, however, an organization may lose sight of the original meaning of the values in its statements of values, charter, mission, or purpose. Without shared values, a complex organization loses the basis for unifying its parts and becomes fragmented. Values in complex human systems must therefore be continually reintegrated because unity of human effort is a product of centering around purpose and values.

Open organizations operate on the basis of two core values: the "worthiness" of outcome goals (desired accomplishments) and the "openness" of process goals (the manner in which those accomplishments will be achieved).

The basis for organizational unity in an open system is a well-defined and *worthy* mission, with an accompanying set of agreed-upon goals. Many goal-setting processes assume a goal will be effective if it is clearly written; however, goals must also be perceived as worthy. They must be felt, embodied, symbolized, and visualized. Effective goal setting not only includes procedures that enable clarity but also contains measures that permit sharing and symbolizing of the underlying values that give meaning to goals.

Open organizations also tend to formulate multidimensional outcome goals, including both survival values and higher being-values that respond to the needs of the environment. That is, they are not simply reducible to a single, quantifiable bottom line. Certainly, effective voluntary and service organizations work toward multidimensional outcomes that enhance the quality of life for their clients and society. In contrast, profit-making organizations depend upon profit as a quantifiable, univariable outcome measure of their effectiveness. Yet even in the private sector, an open organization acknowledges other important values, such as delivery of quality products and services, contributions to the well-being of local communities, maintenance of the natural environment, and funding of cultural or educational enterprises.

For an open organization, *openness* underlies all other values. It is reflected in a tolerance for diversity and creativity in setting and achieving goals. Closed systems often focus on one process value, such as simplicity. This focus might be equated with efficiency, which may lead to a single outcome goal, such as profit. The profit goal may in turn negate high quality. If an organization becomes too focused on single goals or narrow outcomes, it may forfeit systemic thinking and the very processes that produce high-quality products, services, and profits.

Openness as a core value leads to formulation of process goals that account for the developmental needs of workers and of the organization. An excellent example is the unit method of production used by Volvo. In the unit method, the final assembly of a product is done by a single team of people who possess various key technical competencies: electrician, welder, mechanic, and so on. This production method was developed to overcome quality problems that often occur in assembly-line production. The unit method not only satisfies the employees' needs for responsibility, mastery, and pride in their work but also meets the organization's needs for efficient production. A number of other companies, such as Federal Express, Johnson & Johnson, Motorola, Sony, 3M, and Xerox, are known for similarly innovative methods.

Those working to develop open organizations must function primarily as process advocates by modeling and teaching an open-systems approach to diagnosis, communication, problem solving, planning, and evaluation. They must be open-minded, other-oriented, tolerant of ambiguity, and respectful of the organization's culture and values.

Window Two: Congruence. Carl Rogers (1961) defined *congruence* in terms of the degree of overlap between what you are and what you perceive yourself to be. When both are consistent, they reinforce your psychological health. When a large gap exists between them, you live in a state of psychic dissonance. According to Rogers, this gap is painful and, in an attempt to reduce the pain, leads you to distort reality and to engage in dysfunctional behavior. According to Rogers, the road to mental health and well-being is to understand this gap and to learn to accept yourself as you are. You do not need to change to become healthy; you just need to learn how to be what you are. When you live in a state of congruence you know who and what you are and what is being demanded of you in relationships; you are honest with yourself throughout any dialogue, even if it causes you to reflect critically on your assumptions and values.

To fulfill your purpose, you must match opportunity with your desires or goals. You must therefore be aware of your interests and preferences, abilities and capacities, skills, needs and wants, and goals and values. Then you must be able to respond to this data by identifying what needs to be done and knowing how to do it. To achieve balance, you must understand your strengths and limitations and appreciate how to maximize those strengths while accepting and adapting to those limitations.

Window Three: Connection. A caring person seeks connectedness and does so naturally. In *The Art of Loving*, Eric Fromm (1956) defines love or caring in terms of five qualities:

1. Competence to perform one's role.
2. Commitment to the other, the recipient of one's caring.
3. Knowledge of what the other needs.
4. Concentration on the person or group being cared for so that one can correctly provide for its needs.
5. Discipline to do the right thing at the right time.

Each individual member of an organization has a role to fulfill, and this role nurtures some specific outcome. Each individual must understand his or her role and how that role fits into the broad purposes of the whole. In a baseball organization, there is a general manager, a field manager, and twenty-five players. In the best baseball organizations, each role fits together into one seamless whole, with the result that the same organizations tend to win year after year. This teamwork is true of other professional sports and of other types of organizations. To perform effectively, every member must perform his or her role in full awareness of how that role affects the whole. They must make ongoing adjustments to their behavior to ensure that the whole can perform at the highest possible level. Performance in the role must reflect personal concern and caring for others. Connecting requires the capacity to sense what is happening, interpret its meaning properly, adjust your response, check your adjustment, and refine it again and again. In organizations, the person, group, or system is always changing, so to connect with that person, group, or system, you must constantly observe and change or transform yourself as well. Otherwise you cannot provide the connection that is needed.

Window Four: Shared Purpose. Shared purpose binds together the individuals of a group. Without it, there can be no cohesive whole. Shared purpose enhances commitment and meaning and creates powerful synergy — a state in which combined energy and output surpass in quality and quantity the sum of all members' individual energies and resources. Shared purpose provides a common map of reality. It serves as a guide or framework for planning, making decisions, solving problems, evaluating results, making corrections, and so on. A shared purpose reminds the group of its destination. Once a team knows its purpose, it can outline who is responsible for what, detail costs, and know when it has reached its destination.

In a group, shared purpose can truly emerge only when the individuals that make up that group establish congruence between the group's shared purpose and their own value systems and roles. Shared values in the group will emerge only on a basis of trust and subsequent awareness and appreciation of individual differences.

Developing an open organization requires focusing people's energies productively on commonly held purposes and goals. Organizational openness becomes a reality when work groups achieve a team identity based upon shared purpose, goals, objectives or tasks, processes, skills, and ground rules for working together. These agreements provide the context within which the team can exchange information, discover their real purpose, settle power issues, make decisions, and evaluate results. Without a team identity, goals are diverse and work output relatively low. Work output increases as the group achieves internal responsiveness and unity.

Window Five: Quality Relationships. Every group in an organization is a "supplier" to some other group. This "customer" group may be either internal or external to the organization. Each group must identify its customers and their needs, design and create systems to produce products and services that meet those needs, and monitor and improve those systems as needed. That requires coordination of operational activities and interpersonal activities, which in turn requires quality relationships.

Quality relationships are possible only when the people entering into the relationships are reasonably healthy. In other words, they must be capable of entering into and nurturing relationships based on trusting, opening, realizing, and responding to both themselves and others; they must be relatively free of dysfunctional relations; and they must be open to learning.

The organization must also value and support the development of such relationships. Just as the family typically provides the matrix in which individual development unfolds, the organization provides the matrix in which team relationships unfold. When the organization models and encourages open, honest relationships, when it develops routines and rewards that encourage cooperation, it is possible for the team to develop the kinds of relationships required to become a high-performing team.

For team members to develop commitment and become more productive, the team must provide an environment in which its members' deepest needs can be met. Groups must therefore deal with three underlying interpersonal issues: (1) inclusion and acceptance, (2) control, and (3) self-esteem and productivity. When the team enables individuals to meet their need for belonging, power, and competence, then both individuals and the team prosper and succeed.

Window Six: Collaboration. Each group in an organization has a purpose to fulfill—to satisfy certain requirements in the customer-supplier chain. Most work groups are both customers and suppliers. To be good at both roles requires a high degree of upward, downward, and lateral collaboration. As customers, a group must communicate its needs to its suppliers and relay how well suppliers' products and services are meeting these needs. As suppliers, a group needs to identify its customers' needs and determine how well their products and services are meeting those needs.

     Effective collaboration, then, involves the capacity to identify needs correctly and to communicate well with customers and suppliers. It also involves informing customers about available products and services, determining the extent of customer satisfaction, and learning about continuous improvement activities and plans. Quite broadly, collaboration involves being well informed about how your particular function and processes affect the entire organization—even those parts of the organization not directly in the cause-and-effect chain. Effective collaboration also requires sacrifice and generosity. To be effective, collaboration must go beyond the typical quid pro quo.

Window Seven: Shared Vision. In *The Fifth Discipline* (1990, p. 274), Peter Senge says that "without a genuine sense of common vision and values there is nothing to motivate people beyond self-interest." Organizational climates, he says, should be built on merit rather than on politics and games—on "doing what is right" over "who wants what done." Moving beyond an organization's deeply embedded games requires a climate of openness and reflection.

     Peter Block recommends that a vision be strategic—focused on the needs of customers—and lofty—imaginative and engaging. "If your vision statement sounds like motherhood and apple pie and is somewhat embarrassing, you are on the right track" (1987, pp. 109–115).

While top leadership must provide a clear vision for the organization, it must also assist and support groups in creating their own visions. A group vision may be made meaningful by focusing on the group's purpose or mission or on clearly defined tasks. It is vital that these group visions be congruent with the organization's primary vision. A shared vision can be solidified and made "real" by

- Formulating a brief statement of the organization's philosophy in such a way that every person in the organization can express it clearly,
- Developing and initiating policies, procedures, and programs that support it, and
- Communicating the vision in ways that get everyone involved (Sashkin, 1986, pp. 58–61).

Window Eight: Alignment. An organization is a collection of interdependent roles and functions, each contributing to the whole. To survive, make money, attract and retain customers, create a quality work environment, satisfy employees, and contribute to the community and to society as a whole, an organization requires at least the following functions: marketing, financial, operational, and human resources.

A number of subsystems are also needed for a properly functioning whole: a political or decision-making subsystem, a technical subsystem, a cultural subsystem, and a human resource subsystem. All subsystems must work together for the benefit of the whole, which usually requires mutual adjustments. For instance, the technical subsystem must transform inputs and outputs or products and services to bring about a desired outcome or change, the human resource subsystem must provide competent and motivated individuals to run those processes, the cultural subsystem must have routines and rewards in place that reinforce high performance, and the political subsystem must ensure that employees are empowered so that their needs for autonomy and control are satisfied.

Alignment involves understanding how these systems and subsystems interact and making adjustments when they are not in harmony with the whole. It is important to keep in mind, however, that alignment is never absolutely attained; it is an ongoing activity. Effective organizations therefore monitor relevant internal variables as part of their ongoing processes.

Window Nine: Contribution. A primary purpose of any organization is to provide products and services that meet or exceed its customers' expectations. To do so, the organization must:

1. Determine which group or groups of customers they want to serve
2. Understand the needs of their customers
3. Encourage their customers to buy their products and services
4. Learn how the customers are evaluating the products, and respond to those evaluations

Contribution encompasses the ability to perform these four functions. It involves, among other things, collecting and disseminating data about customer needs, disseminating messages that encourage customers to buy, and collecting data about customers' reactions to the products and services provided. However, contribution encompasses more than merely knowing customers; it involves appreciating and understanding the many other factors that can influence the organization's ability to provide quality products and services. Competitors, environmental issues, economic and political conditions, and social concerns, such as equal opportunity, diversity, work-force skill availability, and so on, also influence the organization's ability to respond and succeed. Contribution therefore involves the ability to focus on relevant data, the ability to collect the data, evaluate it, interpret it thoughtfully, and then use it to respond to opportunities.

All of the preceding qualities, dimensions, and levels of an organization make up its internal environment. The successful functioning of this environment, especially alignment of all critical functions and the personal morale of employees constitutes an absolutely necessary condition for delivering quality products and services to an organization's customers in a timely way. The elements of the environment are interdependent.

Interdependence and Interchange

The Open Organization Model views the organization as an energy exchange system comprised of interdependent components. Interdependence is the hallmark of our universe: it does not matter where within the pond a rock is dropped, its very presence will cause ripples across the entire surface. For example, an individual's external responsiveness complements the internal responsiveness of her or his work group. When work group members are highly involved with and concerned for one another (individual external responsiveness), the group's internal responsiveness is high as well. If a group with low internal responsiveness wants to implement a change, its members must become more involved with and committed to the group by seeking awareness of how their inner thoughts and values align with the group's purpose or task.

For an organization to undertake a transformational change, the system's boundaries must be open so that new information may be accessed by all of its parts. Furthermore, the members must be willing to think differently and to expand their schema (their mental view of the world) to include new information and experiences. And they need to be able to reframe their experiences and view the organization differently.

The external environment in which an organization functions often demands changes on all levels: individual, group, and organization. To make appropriate changes, each level must not only know what the other is doing but also respond in a way that produces higher efficiency and effectiveness for all concerned. That can be done only when the organization is open to input from all areas—both internal and external—and everything is discussable.

In a closed organization, the environment is assumed to be stable and individual learning and development may even be discouraged. Life is routine; learning is single-loop (occurring within the system without changing the system itself; see Argyris, 1990; Argyris and Schön, 1974, 1978) or a series of repetitive operations. In a relatively open situation, the organization expects some uncertainty and plans responses to environmental change. And as the environment in which an organization operates becomes more complex and dynamic, the organization's ability to adapt its human and technical resources to change becomes increasingly important.

Opening Organizational Boundaries

To create and tolerate permeable boundaries, an organization must have a clear purpose and shared values, out of which unity may arise. The people of the organization must collaborate to develop internal responsiveness. And the organization's customers and vendors — both internal and external — must be involved in collaboration.

In open organizations, unity and responsiveness are maintained and enhanced by consistently focusing energy on the definition and achievement of vision, purposes, and goals, rather than on power issues. This process brings managers and staff together, participating as equals in planning and implementation, during which trust evolves, individual differences are discovered, and shared values are identified.

When each subsystem is unified and is internally and externally responsive, the organization can take messages in and send them out. This exchange must occur on all levels. The organization can also become aware of mutual causation and can cope effectively by engaging in transformative problem solving, without destruction and chaos. A clear purpose, a trusting climate, and an awareness of individual differences provide self-organizing capacities for the larger system.

As a case in point, an operation within one organization we work with had achieved and maintained high-quality, 100 percent out-of-box performance on one of its products for an extended period. To reduce costs, the company discontinued inspection of incoming component parts obtained from a reliable vendor. Almost simultaneously, the vendor designed and put into production a new part it believed to be superior to the old one. However, the vendor failed to notify the company of the change, had production and quality problems with the new part, and shipped it, running a 27 percent failure rate. Our client put the new part, uninspected, directly into the assembled product and shipped it out. The customers immediately experienced a 27 percent failure rate with a product they had come to expect as 100 percent reliable.

The problem was resolved when the plant manager met with the vendor, in-house quality people, the in-house engineering group, and a consultant who led the task group through a problem-solving process. Openness in data sharing exposed the problem and led to appropriate solutions. The openness to learning made the outcome a success and reestablished the product as 100 percent reliable. What drives this openness is the organization's commitment to maintaining honest relationships with its environment and with its customers and suppliers, both internal and external. Had communications been more open between the company and its vendor, this situation might never have occurred.

Our studies of utility companies have helped us more fully appreciate that internal customer service is just as important as external customer service. We found that internal customers tend to evaluate services in much the same way as external customers. When external customers perceived service quality as negative, internal customers also tended to rate those services negatively. The converse was also true: when external customers rated service as positive, internal customers also tended to rate those services positively.

Not all parts of an open system need be highly responsive to external conditions, however. An assembly line, for example, may function best when it remains closed and well defined, while a research and development unit may alternate between a closed phase of developing products and an open phase of market testing. Similarly, organizations vary in the amount of environmental uncertainty they encounter. Some may experience little outside pressure, while others will be pressured by external forces to adopt a more open strategy in order to be effective. Nevertheless, open systems logic assumes that any organization will be affected to some degree by variables, both internal and external, outside its immediate control. Under conditions of uncertainty, the *capacity* for response, self-maintenance, and self-organization becomes essential.

Summary

The Open Organization Model is a holistic paradigm that (1) optimizes an organization's capacity to allow for the exchange of human energy, (2) minimizes the constraints created by structure, processes, policies, technology, and pressures external to the organization, and (3) is open and communicative both within itself and with other systems in its environment. This model enhances the organization's ability to learn, to adapt, and to respond to a wide variety of environmental jolts and opportunities with incremental or transformative changes.

The model presented here, by virtue of its multidimensional, interdependent nature, is a tool for assessing and explaining the complexities of dynamic organizations. It provides a way for organizations to guide themselves through both incremental, adaptive changes and systemwide transformative change. The Open Organization Model is holistic in that one can enter the system from any level (individual, group, or organization) and still diagnose any of the core dimensions (unity, internal responsiveness, and external responsiveness).

Unity and responsiveness are not achieved at the expense of internal fragmentation or being closed to the environment. Unity and responsiveness permit and promote awareness of self, others, and the external world. These characteristics are the essence of being and becoming, of enabling adaptability, and of having intelligence to manage reality.

THREE

INVOLVING THE WHOLE SYSTEM TO DIAGNOSE, LEARN, AND INITIATE CHANGE

A key task for the learning organization is examining assumptions and encouraging reflective assessment of premises, perspectives, and frames of reference (Mezirow, 1991, p. 5). Unless we become aware of how we subtly repeat the routines we have mastered without thinking about what we wish to accomplish, we produce unintended results. This chapter discusses some basic processes for gathering and applying valid human, strategic, and technical information and for examining systemic interrelationships.

The *diagnostic review* is most applicable for analyzing an organization's strengths and weaknesses at isolated points in time and is especially useful for early diagnosis. *Action research, action science,* and *action learning* can help us access the unconscious thoughts that influence our behaviors on an ongoing basis.

The Diagnostic Review

This diagnostic process is designed to provide a more comprehensive and intensive organizational analysis than other planning and goal-setting processes. A diagnostic review helps answer the following basic questions at any point in time:

- Where are we now? (situational analysis)
- Where do we want to go? (vision, mission, key goals, objectives)
- How do we expect to get there? (strategies, tactics, programs, activities, processes, key shared values)
- What organizational structures are needed? (structure emerges from desired functions)
- Who is going to pay? (budget, revenue sources, markets)
- How will we know when we have arrived? (evaluation processes: context, inputs, processes, products, and impact)

The diagnostic review will demand, on a periodic basis, full staff involvement, written diagnosis and recommendations, and the development of managers' organizational skills. A successful review requires that those involved have a strong sense of ownership and responsibility.

Costs and Benefits of a Review

A diagnostic review is an intense process. Before undertaking one, several issues must be identified and understood.

1. What will such a review cost?
2. What will be the anticipated benefits?
3. Who will be impacted by such a review? Will the review be perceived as a threat? If so, what can be done to ensure that the data will not be discounted? Can something be done to minimize the perception of threat?

(For further information, see Pitman, 1991.)

Goals of a Review

The diagnostic review attempts to integrate sophisticated data collection with joint problem solving, clinical insights, and appropriate action plans. It is designed to enhance and reinforce sharing among leaders and staff and aims to increase communication and agreement about future directions.

Timing a Review

A diagnostic review is appropriate only at critical periods or adaptable moments in the organization's life. It may be precipitated by a crisis, such as a deficit or an unresolved leadership struggle. Or it may be in conjunction with an effort to initiate planned change. It is tailored to supply quick, comprehensive knowledge at major turning points or periods of organizational soul-searching. The need for a diagnostic review is indicated when the organization's leaders have a sense of urgency precipitated by

- Transition from one stage of growth to another
- Sense of unrealized potential
- Mounting deficits, fiscal insolvency, declining profits
- Conflicts about the organization's future direction
- Increasing dissatisfaction with drift and inaction
- Low staff morale, high turnover
- Major changes or jolts in the organization's environment
- Declining appeal of standard services or products
- Retooling to meet new problems or opportunities
- New leaders desiring to take new approaches

Completing the analysis may take from one to several months from the time the review is initiated until the summary report is presented. The period should be timed to maintain momentum and timely recommendations. Because of its depth and breadth, a thorough diagnostic review is unsuitable more often than every two to four years; however, brief annual updating may be desirable.

Roles for a Review

We recommend that an external consultant facilitate the review, with broad participation of leaders, constituents, and members of the organization. All participants must reserve time and energy for this process. A group formed of both internal and external people takes on the role of an Action Research Team.

This team *must take a systemic view*. The team interviews others in depth, and prepares reports and recommendations in consultation with leaders. Follow-up activities then take place amidst full and open discussion. This approach views the organization as having the capability to identify its own needs and discover the best ways to fulfill them.

Knowledgeable staff members often join external consultants to conduct the study; however, in-house members should implement all action plans. The consultant may conduct training and act as a "shadow consultant," but should under no conditions upstage or replace existing leadership.

The consultant's role in a diagnostic review differs from that of a consulting firm retained to provide expert answers. Outside expertise may aid diagnosis, but much of the review process involves crystallizing and applying the organization's latent wisdom. It must be kept in mind that no scientific study or consultation aid can replace the collective experience of people who work inside the organization.

Managers also play a critical role in this process. First, they must be willing to act on the data collected through the review. Second, managers significantly influence the perceptions and behaviors of those around them. Feedback, especially upward performance appraisal, tends to equalize the sense of power at various levels of the organization (Chase, 1968) because it leads to increased dialogue and learning across hierarchical levels and reduces fear. Greater involvement of supervisors, managers, and leaders in the feedback process tends to result in greater satisfaction and greater perceived use of survey data (Klein, Kraut, and Wolfson, 1971; Hauser, Pecorella, and Wissler, 1975). Antagonistic authority figures can undermine the review process.

Stages of a Review

The diagnostic review corresponds to the six phases in the consulting process identified by Lippitt and Lippitt (1978).

1. Initial entry—developing consensus about ways in which a diagnostic study may help satisfy the organization's needs and outlining a tentative plan.

2. Formulating a contract and establishing a helping relationship — defining and agreeing on the consulting relationship,
   objectives for the study, the activities to be performed, and
   the time and cost for services.
3. Problem identification, diagnostic analysis, and recommendations — collecting, organizing, and analyzing information
   through individual structured interviews of key people in
   the organization. The findings are analyzed in terms of an
   open systems model and summarized in a written report.
   Areas of strength and weakness are identified, as are discrepancies between present realities and desired goals. Finally, various options for action are explored and specific
   actions recommended.
4. Goal setting and planning — discussion and planning based
   on the review summary, reaching joint agreement on needs
   and goals, and evaluating and revising plans.
5. Taking action and cycling feedback — orchestrating and
   monitoring change by
   • Continuing development of alternatives and possible so-
     lutions to specific problems
   • Developing skills to enable people to take necessary ac-
     tions
   • Establishing procedures to elicit feedback on progress
   • Promoting operational flexibility to deal with unex-
     pected problems
   • Using feedback to reexamine goals and strategies
6. Contract completion: continuity, support, and termina-
   tion — phasing out the external consultant when immediate goals for improvement are achieved and independent
   leadership and data-based feedback processes are established. At this point, trained Action Research Teams continue the process of data-based action planning and implementation.

We will now move on to the processes that can help bring
about critical reflection on underlying assumptions and transformational learning after diagnosis: action learning, action
science, and action research.

Action Learning

The concepts of transformational learning (Mezirow, 1991), accommodation (Piaget, 1980), and double-loop learning (Argyris and Schön, 1974) address the same critical process as action learning: reflection on the ways in which our context, values, goals, and experiences influence our perceptions. When people do not apply action learning (or reflective learning) skills, they tend to operate by trial and error. However, when they reexamine their strategies and the governing values that influence those strategies, they can adjust the gap between where they are and where they want to be.

We all have learning histories that shape how we view the world and influence how we operate in various environments. When we become really skilled at something, the cognitive process required for the particular operation leaves our conscious awareness. When that happens, our preexisting competencies may create barriers that interfere with solving new problems and overcoming new challenges.

These barriers to learning may lead to what Chris Argyris (1986) calls "skilled incompetence" or may activate defensive routines (Argyris, 1990), which can undermine our effectiveness and create hardships for ourselves and those who try to help us. In stressful situations, we tend to repeat those behaviors that worked in the past, but they may not apply to the present situation. The lack of critical reflection often prevents us from implementing necessary changes. Action science offers some potential answers to these problems.

Action Science

Action science is an intensive learning and problem-solving process developed by Argyris and Schön (1974) through which individuals can discover how they produce unintended results or unconsciously help create problematic situations. Action science theory and methods are founded on several key principles.

Principle 1. Our behaviors are based upon our implicit theories of reality. This principle asserts that all actions stem from our assumptions—both individual and collective—about what is *real,* what is important and worth striving for (what we *value*), and what is *possible* in the reality we perceive. The concept of attribution clarifies the effects of these implicit theories. Attributions are explanations or theories we create to help us understand events and make them more predictable. These explanations may or may not be accurate, but we may not know that because we do not often test the validity of our explanations. Instead, we assume our attributions are correct. One problem leaders encounter is that people tend to act on their attributions as if they were true, without data to confirm or reject them. As a result, people often behave based on assumptions that are invalid at best and entirely false at worst. Action science is a tool for testing the connections between attributions and reality and for changing attributions that are shown to be false.

Principle 2. Our actions tend to be consistent with our theories. Our implicit theories are self-fulfilling in the sense that actions conform to assumptions. Action science helps uncover the theories that guide our decision making and problem solving and the assumptions they are based on, which often lie outside conscious awareness. By uncovering these theories, we can better test their validity and discover the root causes of problems.

Principle 3. Our implicit theories of action tend to be unconscious. Because our theories tend to lie outside conscious awareness, we often make decisions, solve problems, develop and implement plans, and allocate resources on the basis of assumptions that may or may not be valid. The action taken can then produce a result different from the result that is desired and necessary. That action is thus not productive, counterproductive, or at best only partially productive, and output requirements are not met. When people encounter and label a situation, they do so at various levels of abstraction. The next section describes four levels of abstraction.

The Ladder of Inference

Chris Argyris (1990) uses a concept called the "Ladder of Inference" to explain how assumptions and attributions, rather than data, inform decision making. The Ladder of Inference has four levels:

1. Directly observable data—what was actually said or done. This data might be a transcript or recording of a conversation or it might be one's recollection of what went on. On this level, feelings as well as actual behavior and dialogue could be considered data.
2. Culturally understood meanings—the way most people from the same culture would interpret directly observable data. Individuals from different cultures, even when located in the same geographic location, may interpret the same data differently. This applies to the different sexes as well.
3. We impose meanings on directly observable data and make attributions, guided by theories on level four that attempt to make sense of or interpret directly observable data.
4. Theories used to create those meanings—the internal and often undiscussable reasoning we use to interpret the world. Note that this reasoning *is not necessarily flawed* or illogical; however, it may be based on inaccurate assumptions or interpretations that have not been confirmed or refuted.

Most of us operate at level 4, using our theories to explain the behavior of others. However, these theories are often invalid. Often, we do not know our theories-in-use. We operate from our espoused theories—the theories we are aware of and can describe. The gap between espoused theories and theories-in-use can be the source of grave problems for an organization. They can lead to further gaps between intended results and actual results. Examination of such gaps, however, can be a powerful tool for continuous learning.

The Ladder of Inference can help us visualize the level of abstraction at which our theories operate and help us understand why many theory-based actions do not produce the intended results. Let us therefore take a closer look at espoused theories versus theories-in-use.

Espoused Theories Versus Theories-in-Use

Espoused theories are theories we are aware of and can state: what we consciously intend, what we give allegiance to, and what we say we do. When asked how we would behave under certain circumstances, we answer based on our espoused theory. However, those theories that truly govern our actions are *theories-in-use* — common assumptions about self, others, and the situation and the connections among action, consequence, and the situation. Espoused theories may or may not be consistent with theories-in-use. In fact, some degree of incongruence is common.

Theories-in-use involve an interrelated set of tacit propositions that guide our behavior in different situations. Each of us has many theories-in-use — one for every situation in which we regularly find ourselves. When people know how to behave in a given situation to achieve what they intend, they know what their theory-in-use is for that situation. They are aware of the result they wish to attain, they know what action is appropriate in that situation, and they know what assumptions are contained in their theories.

However, in most situations people do *not* know their theory-in-use. We cannot learn about other people's theories-in-use by simply asking. We must discern such theories by observing their behaviors. By the same token, we ourselves are usually not conscious of our own theories-in-use. We do not always see how our values and goals influence our behavior and what impact that has on others. We cannot always discern the link between our actions and unintentional results. People are often blind to their actual degree of ineffectiveness as perceived by others.

The incongruence that often exists between an espoused theory and a theory-in-use may have many sources, but whatever its cause, reeducation is a must. The first step is analyzing and defining patterns of existing theories-in-use.

By publicly testing the theories that guide personal practice, we can begin to discover what to change in order to prevent unintended outcomes. To test our theories-in-use, we must confront our own defensiveness, the defensiveness of others, and the ineffectiveness of the group. Working through the thought processes and discussing possibilities with the people involved can bring many new insights. The use of action science allows work groups to minimize actions that produce unintentional results.

When people and organizations reduce the discrepancies between what they *say* drives their behavior and what actually *does,* they are in a powerful position to undertake deep change. Only then will they be able to examine clearly their vision, goals, values, norms, and their underlying assumptions.

With action science, an outside observer records dialogue in a particular situation and then analyzes it. When this analysis is shared, it gives the people in a relationship a bird's-eye view of how they behave. It provides them with information they can use to gain new interpersonal insights through redesign and on-line practice.

Action science, properly applied, is a practical model of meta-learning and it can

- help uncover new approaches to previously unsolved problems.
- help make it possible to discuss the undiscussable.
- help measure and improve the communication skills of individuals in an organization.
- provide a method whereby persons involved in a problematic interaction that has produced poor or unintended results can discover and modify the theories-in-use or assumptions that have led to those results.

The Action Research Process

When people do not stop to consider whether the results they produce match their intentions, they often get caught in single-loop, plan-do, plan-do, plan-do cycles, without examining what is happening or making adjustments along the way. Action research offers a way of breaking such cycles.

Action research (sometimes referred to as continuous improvement or PDCA — Plan-Do-Check-Act) is a consciously directed, cyclical process through which people problem solve following clearly defined phases. These phases include defining a problem, analyzing its probable causes, reaching mutual agreement about potential solutions, testing those solutions by taking action, collecting and analyzing data on the results of the action taken, and repeating the process, making continual adjustments in light of feedback until satisfactory results are achieved. The information collected during one action cycle helps guide action in the next.

As a formal approach, action research was pioneered in the late 1940s by Kurt Lewin (1946), a social scientist interested in the development of data-based feedback. Lewin recognized that problems were being tackled before progress standards had been set for measuring results. He deplored time wasted in futile efforts that were tossed aside with no attempt by innovators to learn from their achievements or failures. Lewin believed that the only good theory is a practical theory and that action research could bridge the gap. He examined action in two steps: (1) investigation of laws contributing to theory and practice and (2) diagnosis of a situation leading to solving a particular problem.

In place of such steps, we recommend the Plan-Do-Check-Act (PDCA) model, favored by quality improvement planners. Using the PDCA cycle, the organization compares the results it is getting, reviews the effectiveness of its effort, and improves on its methods throughout the change process. Quality consultant Ron Crosling of Melbourne, Australia, illustrates the PDCA cycle, as shown in Figure 3.1.

In addition to these steps, action research also includes examining a process or a model, analyzing whether it is working optimally, and then determining whether changes should be made. Thus the model itself *and* the results achieved are continually observed and evaluated.

To enhance our effectiveness, we must understand our behaviors, which entails understanding the theories behind our behaviors. To reach our full potential, we must monitor our behavior while in the process of achieving our goals (Argyris and Schön, 1974, p. xi). That can be accomplished in part through the observations of others by Action Research Teams, Such a team can form a community that supports individual learning through critical reflection or analysis of values, assumptions, premises, and frames of reference. Such variables may either limit or enhance individual and group learning.

Figure 3.1. Plan-Do-Check-Act.

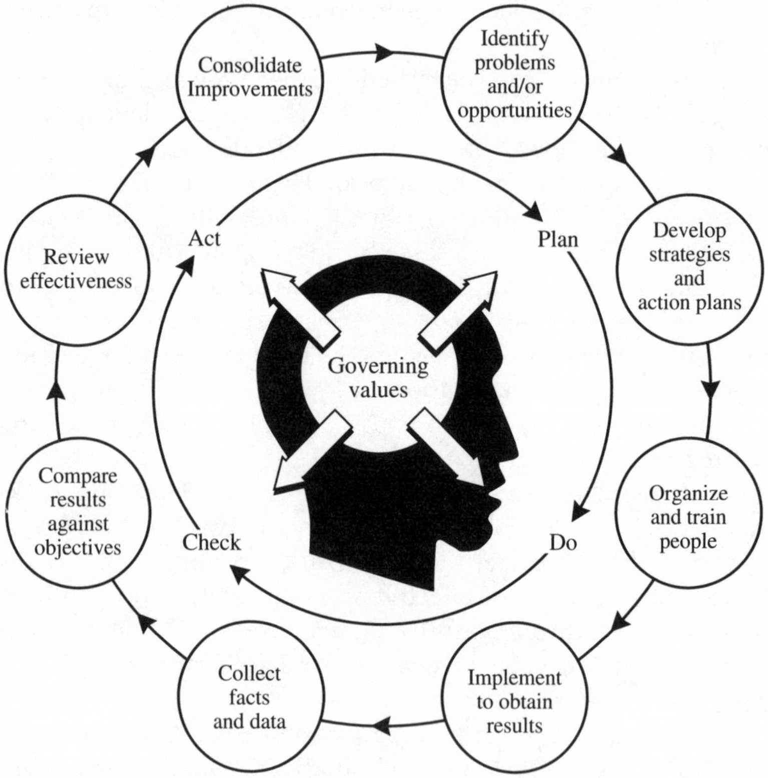

Source: Courtesy of Ron Crosling.

The Action Research Team

The Action Research Team (ART) is a special type of team designed to build feedback and problem solving into organizational structures. It is an important locus within which organizational openness is practiced in daily operations. This team provides a mechanism for weighing emerging concerns and problems in the organization and allows for continuous improvement and transformative learning while the change is taking place. By applying a scientific approach to the change process,

ARTs can generate alternative solutions and determine the best changes and strategies for coping with concerns, all through a collaborative framework within the organizational structure. The team assists in resolving problems in the whole system as well as those specific to particular units. Through systematic diagnosis, planning, implementation, and evaluation, ARTs themselves become a collection of agents leading change.

Establishing an ART also directly addresses a problem common to many modern organizations: the perceived lack of responsiveness to goals, energies, capabilities, and employee needs. Such a lack of responsiveness is not a conscious effort on the part of leaders to deny employees self-fulfillment. It is a by-product of modern society and of organizational customs and culture. Use of an ART begins to provide for individual needs, particularly the need to understand and adjust to change throughout an organization.

We have found that the cross-functional, multilevel group with a clear charter is the most effective type of Action Research Team. It is helpful if the group's purpose or goal is some systemic performance indicator, such as meeting a research and development deadline or reducing production reject rates to a set level. Once a clear purpose has been established, the team forms. An in-house manager whose role is crucial to the effort should serve as a team member, and someone external to all the functions should facilitate. A team leader should also be identified or designated. When the team has formed, training in the action research process begins.

When an ART is functioning, the chances increase that change will be accepted. First, those most affected by the change will have been involved in planning for the change and will have gained commitment to it. They will be much more likely to understand, accept, and act upon changes when they have helped to collect data, identify pressing problems, and work through options for resolving those problems. Second, human resources will be used in interesting, new, and challenging ways. Skills lying dormant will be called upon. New skills may need to be learned. Team members learn new group processes while working on real problems, thereby stimulating individual learning.

Thus, the two kinds of change become synergistic and form a basis for a learning climate. In such a climate, discourse can begin to validate the definition and solution of problems.

Ensuring Team Effectiveness

An effective ART is built on certain assumptions. One is that there is a recognized need for change. A second is that there will be systematic data collection to diagnose causes of problems and dissatisfaction and to set goals. Still another is that it is possible to devise group action to achieve goals. It is assumed that new ideas will come from the interplay of research and action, once new and better data are collected and analyzed.

The successful use of Action Research Teams can result in several valuable outcomes:

- Implementation of systemwide change programs
- Progressive resolution of chronic operational problems
- Identification of emerging concerns
- Confronting and working through differences
- Increased worker involvement in change and learning
- Increased worker skills in group processes and problem solving

Through the cyclical process of action research, the ART strives continuously to improve everyday operations and the organization's environment. If this process is to work effectively, certain features must be present: client-consultant collaboration, internal resource development, the interplay of research and action, [individual and group learning at the transformative level], and continuous monitoring and evaluation (Frohman, Sashkin, and Kavanagh, 1976).

Starting an Action Research Team

This section describes how an ART typically starts. The process of setting up an ART and working through an initial problem involves four phases: entry into the organization, start-up, action interventions, and evaluation.

Phase One: Entry into the Organization

Authority and Impact. The ART has no formal power unless management chooses to give it power. When Action Research Teams are self-appointed, they enjoy high member interest and energy; however, they may have difficulty acquiring resources, countering management suspicion, blending into prevailing structures, and gaining access to existing power. On the other hand, when ARTs are created by top management, they have a link to formal power, a definite mandate for action, a defined role, and a ready framework for achieving change. But they may be viewed as a tool of management, greeted with suspicion and hostility, and hampered by too little commitment to the task. The advantages and disadvantages of appointed versus volunteer teams must be weighed in relation to the organization's particular situation.

When management establishes an ART, they identify an issue of concern and announce it through an official vehicle of the organization. Next, vice presidents (or executives one authority level below the chief executive) present the ART concept to their managerial subordinates or key functional groups or to cross-functional groups that are already operating. This process is followed along the authority structure until every employee has received information about the ART. These actions sanction and legitimize the ART as a function of the organization. Finally, the chief executive and key staff develop team-selection criteria.

Phase Two: Start-up

Team Selection. ARTs work best when members have a real interest in serving, an aptitude for working in groups, a high trust level already established, an investment in the organization, a healthy personality, good communication skills, and an established membership in an informal communication network.

For a high level of energy and involvement, interest in serving should take precedence over ensuring a representative group. Ideally, however, an ART should have representatives from all organization areas affected by a change. For systemwide change, a team should have representatives from all constituents. The nature of the task, available technology, goals, and the kind of change (first- or second-order) all influence the composition of the ART.

In a corporation, a team would include a top executive, middle managers, and workers. A team in a small college would include a dean, department chairperson, and faculty. However, for change primarily affecting an individual work unit, the team could be composed of representatives of management, work teams in the unit, and perhaps key groups that interface with the work unit. In a small department, each person might be a member, and action research would be used as one of several methods to do work.

Team Development. Team building is an ongoing process. Team building is scheduled, preferably in one or two large time blocks, to develop group identity, trust, shared values and norms, and mechanisms for maintenance and renewal. This initial step is crucial to ensure team cohesion when working with others to solve problems.

Team Training. Training is also an ongoing process that begins during the start-up phase. We have found that the initial training requires at least three days or twenty-four hours of clock time. Members begin by learning one another's skills and areas of interest. They assess resources already available in the group and skills they want to acquire. They may request training in several areas.

Problem Definition. Although the issue was initially stated by top management, the ART must define the problem and its ramifications and establish ownership through its own analysis. The definition can change as more information becomes available.

Summarized Evaluation Plan. The ART develops a plan to evaluate the impact of its intervention at the conclusion of the change process. Design meetings may be open to all or part of the organization, depending on the intensity and complexity of the activity and on the availability of resources.

Documentation. Experience has shown that it is essential for the ART to document in detail all actions taken and diagnostics applied in order to track everything that happens. Without such a record, valuable information may be lost.

Phase Three: Action Interventions

Baseline Data Collection. Data-based feedback and problem solving are important to an organization's adaptability. The ART collects information about the problem situation it has identified. It may use interviews, surveys, observations, and questionnaires to gather data. During this process, the challenges of direct communications must be considered.

The feelings of the people from whom data will be collected must also be taken into account. Many people are threatened by data-collection and evaluation activities, particularly when they are unfamiliar with the concepts and techniques. Some people experience fears of inadequacy and incompetence; others may be concerned about the possibility of increased workload. Given these concerns, it is important that data be collected in an open and trusting atmosphere. If data are to be collected in a group setting, it is helpful to do some group development processes beforehand. These include but are not limited to: clarifying purpose, developing trust, establishing individual differences, providing feedback, establishing a protocol for problem solving, and establishing a process for celebrating successes and mourning failures. In addition, members of the group may need training in data analysis, communication across function and hierarchical levels, and critical reflection.

It is always important to get multiple perspectives about a change effort. During both the planning of a change and the interpretation of data, action research should include people who will be affected by the change for two primary reasons: accuracy of raw and interpreted data and acceptance of the process by the people it affects. The complexity of the problem will determine the diversity and competence level needed from the group. The individuals can provide the multiple perspectives necessary. However, change facilitators are well advised to involve skeptics in the assessment process because they can raise questions and uncover critical problems that might otherwise be overlooked. When skeptical individuals are an integral part of the problem-solving process, they are also less likely to become negative influences that hinder the change effort (see Mohrman and Cummings, 1989).

Analysis and Feedback. The ART analyzes the data and prepares a report summarizing the conclusions. Depending on the problem, the team holds small or large group meetings to present its conclusions and to solicit questions and comments from others.

Problem Redefinition. At this point the ART has gathered sufficient new and reinterpreted information to allow for problem restatement or problem refinement. It *must* stop to check for congruency before progressing to the next step.

Action Planning. The ART sets goals and criteria for successful achievement. It generates alternative strategies for achieving the goals and selects the most promising one. Then the ART designs an action plan that includes objectives, activities, evaluation criteria, and an evaluation method to judge whether the plan is working as intended.

Implementation. After the plan has had sufficient time to be tried, its implementation is evaluated. Based on collected data, the plan is continued, revised, or terminated. The plan may be reevaluated and revised at several checkpoints during implementation.

Phase Four: Evaluation

Summarized Data Collection. At this point the ART administers instruments to collect baseline data for a second time. This information will be compared with data collected in phase three to evaluate the impact of the ART's intervention.

Analysis and Feedback. The ART analyzes data and prepares a comprehensive report. After meeting with the strategic planning staff to present the findings and obtain questions and comments, the ART revises the action plan as needed.

Transfer of Responsibility. Finally, the ART plans for transfer of responsibility to the appropriate organizational structures (temporary or more permanent), after which the team will leave this particular concern and focus on another.

Summary

A thorough diagnostic review provides a way to get people talking about an organization's problems, growth areas, and goals. It raises awareness of discrepancies between the present situation and what people want their organization to become. A diagnostic review clarifies values, renews purpose, sets goal priorities, and motivates change toward openness. This intensive process is suitable for both early diagnosis and periodic follow-up.

Action research and action science provide for the ongoing monitoring and adjusting that openness and continuous improvement require. Both typically involve action learning so that the relevance and validity of the system's governing values and ideals can be examined. Action research helps people consciously analyze the problems they face, identify the causes of those problems, reach mutual agreement about potential solutions, and test those solutions by taking action and making adjustments as required. Action science provides ways to access, observe, and analyze unconscious behaviors that may be contributing to problem situations. It can open the door to critical reflection on influential variables outside of conscious awareness, making our experiences more accessible and discussable.

To ensure that these processes have the most valuable effect, we recommend the use of Action Research Teams. These should be cross-functional teams with specific charters to scientifically study and help address problems and opportunities, in collaboration with other organizational components.

PART TWO:
A GUIDE FOR CHANGE

FOUR

ADDRESSING ORGANIZATION-WIDE ISSUES: THE CASE OF PRECISION GRINDING AND MANUFACTURING

Chapters Four through Nine demonstrate how the Open Organization Model can serve as a framework and guide for developing a comprehensive transformation strategy. These case study chapters illustrate the ways in which individual and group performance connect to customer service and satisfaction. Figure 4.1 provides a graphic representation of these interconnections. (Note the diagonal running through windows one, five, and nine.) The case study in this chapter and the next describes an intervention at the organization level at a company called Precision Grinding and Manufacturing.

Some Historical Perspective

Precision Grinding and Manufacturing (PGM) is a world-class parts supplier based in Rochester, New York. The company manufactures unique machined parts for computer, office machine, medical, automotive, and military industries. Its well-established product line includes special printer hammers, cutting edge instruments, carbon heart valves, microsurgical scissors, trigger housing groups, cam phaser assemblies, chassis assemblies, shell connectors, and so on. PGM's customers include

Figure 4.1. Interconnectedness in the Open Organization Model.

	Unity	Internal responsiveness	External responsiveness
Individual	1 **Values**	2 Congruence	3 Connection
Group	4 Shared purpose	5 **Quality relationships**	6 Collaboration
Organization	7 Shared vision	8 Alignment	9 **Contribution**

IBM, Xerox, General Electric, Digital Equipment Corporation, Wang, CarboMedics, Eastman Kodak, General Motors, RCA, Bendix Aerospace, and Beretta.

The president of PGM, Bill Hockenberger (known by his employees as "Hock"), started the company in the basement of his house in 1967 with an old machine tool he bought and rebuilt. Hockenberger places a high value on challenge, diversity, and growth. From the start, the company sought the most difficult machining jobs available. The precision of the parts that PGM produces can be measured in ten-thousandths or millionths of an inch.

Although the firm had a long history of profitable operation, it began experiencing difficulties. Competition was increasing, and PGM was losing contracts to foreign suppliers. Not only was it losing new contracts, but also it was struggling to keep the customers it had. PGM's rate of sales had remained about the same but overhead had increased tremendously. The ever-changing technology required extensive capital investments in new manufacturing equipment. And customers were demanding lower prices. The company's profit margin began to shrink, and PGM began to worry about its survival.

PGM had about 110 employees when Hockenberger hired a manufacturing expert to help "put the organization on its feet." This man had a good reputation for running small businesses. When he came on board, he divided the company, which had been previously organized into small project groups, into various functional specialties. He fired some people whose productivity and leadership were highly questionable and hired new people to fill such roles as vice president of engineering, vice president of manufacturing, and so on. However, this reorganization failed to produce the intended results and the business continued to decline.

Discovering the Problem

When we began our work with PGM, about three years after the change from project groups to functional areas was made, the company was clearly operating in a reactive mode. Its leaders were spending most of their time responding to problems and crises that resulted from poor planning and were trying to stay afloat. While their goals had once emphasized innovation and creativity, they now revolved around stability and consistency. To be accepted, changes had to be slow and incremental. Employees were so focused on solving short-term, urgent problems and overcoming obstacles that they could not think about the future. Despite a verbal commitment to marketing, the company had no written marketing plan. PGM was at the mercy of its external environment.

PGM's people were enmeshed in doing more of the same and were not learning from these experiences. Our challenge was to help them shift from this reactive stance to a strategic-creative mindset. Table 4.1 summarizes the nature of the required changes by comparing and contrasting six major differences between reactive and strategic-creative mindsets.

In that PGM's primary goal was to attract and retain customers, one of our first tasks was to identify why customers were leaving, which was not a simple endeavor. When we asked who

Table 4.1. Reactive Versus Strategic-Creative Mindsets.

	Reactive (First-Order) Mindset	Strategic-Creative (Second-Order) Mindset
Orientation	Maintain status quo	Determine what is wanted
Primary goal	Stability, consistency	Alignment, empowerment
Attitude toward change	Slow and incremental change	Discontinuous change is okay
Time perspective	Short term, urgent	Long term, patient
Emphasis	Problem solve and overcome obstacles	Focus on desired results
Source of control	External environment	Inner world

PGM's customers were, we discovered that the organization really did not know. No good records about customers and customer needs and expectations existed. The company tended not to pursue previous customers. Rather, it waited until a new customer approached them to ask for a bid, or an old one offered new business. It would then produce a new bid. A new marketing group had been formed, but it was totally neglecting what was once known about PGM's customers. All previous information had been lost. One department blamed another for losing customers—all along the line. Engineers and production people blamed sales and marketing people for not doing a good job. The net result of this infighting was that customer needs were not being met, and they became disenchanted and began abandoning the company.

However, the situation at PGM was not all bad. The company was and is very strong in grinding, machining, and finishing methodologies and uses state-of-the-art measuring devices to ensure consistent quality products. Its ability to provide such a high level of quality put it in a unique marketing position with enormous potential for growth.

When we first looked inside the organization, PGM was one of the cleanest job shops or production shops we had ever seen. The firm's facility, equipment, and staff were significantly superior to most machine shops of that size. It was an organization of top-notch machinists and engineers who could take on truly difficult tasks and do an excellent job. They had tremendous talent and a tremendous track record.

Before the reorganization, PGM had performed its work in small groups and project teams that typically consisted of a journeyman machinist, an engineer, and others as needed. But when the business reorganized into functional areas, conflicts immediately evolved, with engineers fighting manufacturing people, and both of these groups fighting with sales representatives, and so on. In addition, along with the reorganization came inevitable downsizing. These changes had led to low morale and high levels of dissatisfaction. Hockenberger was troubled by what seemed to be an even lower level of employee commitment to PGM.

As we studied this company, a hypothesis began to emerge: it appeared that the new bureaucratic culture of functional units, introduced by the manufacturing expert in charge of the reorganization, directly conflicted with the culture that had built PGM and made it successful. People were not prepared for functional leadership roles. They did not understand how they worked. They needed both experience and education to make these new jobs work.

Such specialization might be effective when it is congruent with the organization's culture and values. But, as a rule, the greater the interdependence among organizational tasks, the more difficult it is to deal with those tasks through departmentalization (Scott, 1987). And at PGM, and many other companies, marketing, design, engineering, and production tend to be highly interdependent. So the new structure only compounded the problems of working together toward shared goals.

While the old organization had once been very good at personal follow-up with customers, the level of follow-up had declined rapidly after the reorganization. The old project teams had been very responsive to their particular set of customers and had worked closely with them. In the functionally aligned organization, however, no one was taking the initiative to follow up with customers, and, as a result, customers were falling through the cracks. No one person seemed to be truly committed to meeting the expectations of key customers.

Because PGM's people were divided over the whole reorganization, they were enmeshed in determining who was most important rather than focused on the goal of satisfying customer needs. They were more concerned about who was the top engineer and who was the next one. Old friends were now in bitter conflict. Everyone felt insecure.

Determining a Strategy

The principal task of our intervention was twofold: (1) to restore the organic nature of the original organization — the matrix-like culture of interdisciplinary task teamwork and working with a particular customer on a particular product line — and (2) to move the organization from its reactive stance toward a high-performance orientation. Among the intents of our intervention were to help PGM:

- Set up a flexible, task-oriented organization, with proven team leaders in key positions.
- Put people in positions that matched their strengths, thus strengthening the company.
- Eliminate unnecessary positions that hampered a task-oriented, team-run organization.
- Reduce indirect labor expense and bring the direct-to-indirect labor ratio in line and keep it there.
- Create an atmosphere that fostered continuous improvement, ownership, and a drive to be the best in the industry.

Executive Team Development

We began our intervention by helping PGM's leaders pull together as an executive team through "strategic team development." A highly motivated, trained, and totally open management team can do much to create a productive atmosphere, and strategic team development has proved an effective strategy for developing such teams. Top management's commitment to a continuous improvement plan is crucial for eliminating constraints on employee performance. Strategic team development involves the following steps:

- Developing vision, mission, and values
- Developing strategy and goals
- Clarifying roles and working relationships
- Developing and aligning structure
- Working together

This general model provided the structure for our intervention.

Working closely with PGM's leaders, we analyzed the company's strengths and weaknesses and its opportunities and threats (SWOTs). Seminars were held to teach supervisory theory and concepts as well as skills to help develop and manage an open organization (which was more like Hockenberger's original firm). We reviewed the need for management development and guided the leaders through role negotiations and helped them evaluate PGM's policies and procedures.

We overviewed the group process and discussed the need for collaboration, for getting people together and exchanging views and ideas. Company leaders began promoting an attitude of "We're in this together: get help, give help, and have fun working together."

We suggested ways that management could create an environment where people felt like participating and could apply their natural ability and creativity. The need to take intelligent risks was discussed. The executive team adopted the philosophy that it was okay to make mistakes; as long as people learned from them, there would be no reprisals.

We reviewed the importance of maintaining open and honest communication and of ensuring that each employee had a clear understanding of the company's values, vision, mission, and goals. We stressed that communication partly involves making certain you are understood and that it is important to speak up and share thoughts and feelings as issues. It is also important to give others your undivided attention and to hear them out.

The issue of trust was also addressed. We underscored the importance of doing what you say and pointed out that keeping commitments builds integrity, credibility, and respect. Finally, we emphasized celebrating victories. Any victory, regardless of size or importance, should be enjoyed and shared.

Examining PGM's Values, Vision, Mission, and Goals

From these discussions and a number of written exercises, PGM's executive team formulated formal company values, vision, and mission statements and articulated company goals. These statements reflect the team's renewed people orientation and restored PGM's old philosophy that viewed highly competent people as the most crucial factor for success.

PGM's Company Values.
- *People:* Treating and recognizing people as our most important resource.
- *Teamwork:* Working together to achieve our goals and realize our vision where open and honest confrontation is encouraged with everything being expressible and discussable.
- *Integrity:* Acting consistent with our values: treating everyone with respect, fairness, and honesty.
- *Adaptability:* Being open to and analyzing new concepts, processes, materials, and tools in order to benefit from opportunities to obtain new business and perform with greater efficiency and effectiveness, both internally and externally.
- *Excellence:* Giving our customers and associates unsurpassed value in our products, services, and relationships.
- *Achievement:* Attaining results through initiative, creativity, and perseverance.
- *Work environment:* Maintaining safe and clean facilities and equipment. An open management system that encourages individualized efforts and decision making. A continuous learning environment.

PGM's Vision. An international, multidivisional organization responding to the world's manufacturing challenges with superior solutions and products created by a family of talented people, each offering their unique ideas and skills in an open, secure environment, where each has a voice.

An uncompromising dedication to quality and excellence in our products and personal relationships coupled with a continual determination to offer the marketplace and society a better way.

PGM's Mission. We specialize in offering customers difficult-to-source parts and assemblies, made with superior quality, delivered on time, with a reasonable contribution to the profitability of our company.

PGM's Goals. PGM's long-term goal aims toward expansion. The company targeted an increase in annual sales from $8 million when our intervention started to $12 million by 1995. The following are the executive team's overall goal statements:

- To provide superior quality, on-time delivery, and competitive pricing in our products and services so we are recognized by our customers as a premier firm concerned with their needs.
- To form and support a high-performance organization, thereby providing secure employment with a higher quality work life for our people.
- To develop and promote learning opportunities to enable our people to meet and overcome future challenges with superior solutions and technologies.
- To create, implement, and maintain marketing and capital investment plans to strengthen and broaden our customer base and to manage capacity to meet demand.

In addition, PGM established a long-term goal of designing and producing its own products.

Applying the Strategy
Through Action Research Teams

Once we had completed our initial work with PGM's executive team, it became an Action Research Team for strategic planning. We then helped form four other ARTs: marketing, bidding and finances, engineering-manufacturing, and human resources.

Marketing

The marketing ART recommended that an annual written marketing plan serve as a working document to guide PGM's overall marketing efforts. The plan would include PGM's mission statement and marketing goals, as determined by senior management. Strategic direction regarding product line, pricing, promotion, and distribution would be outlined. The plan would also supply marketing strategies, actions, and tactics to ensure the achievement of corporate sales goals, including strategies for geographic market expansion. An action plan would also be created so the company would be prepared for an economic downturn.

PGM decided to devote more energy to maintaining its reputation as a high-quality, reliable supplier. It set a goal to become and remain the preferred supplier to both new and existing customers. More emphasis was placed on determining and meeting the real (fit for use) functional needs of customers. PGM developed a formal system to obtain customer feedback on the company's performance, which involved a questionnaire and a data base for recording feedback.

Because the company valued variety and challenge, it decided to increase product diversification, particularly in the medical industry. To ensure further financial stability, it set a long-term goal of having no more than 25 percent of sales come from the same company or industry.

As part of its long-term goal of expansion, the company decided to develop potential customers in geographic areas where it already had established representatives. In addition, representatives would be developed in geographic areas with potential future customers and opportunities.

Finances

Marketing and finance worked in concert to sort the company's existing and potential customers into two basic types: the favored market and the fill-in market. The favored market stressed challenging projects in a job-shop atmosphere — PGM's traditional type of work. The fill-in market emphasized quick, light, simple engineering products — jobs that could provide a steady cash flow. This decision allowed PGM to take on creative projects yet maintain a positive cash flow for covering debts and financing quality people. In addition, these consistent sources of capital allowed the company to take advantage of new business opportunities. Other concerns the financial ART addressed included developing criteria for distribution of pretax profits (through profit sharing and gain sharing) and developing an objective method for measuring productivity.

Manufacturing and Engineering

A primary task for the manufacturing and engineering ART was to increase the integration between the manufacturing, engineering, and quality functions, as well as between those areas and marketing and sales. For instance, marketing and engineering people needed to work more closely to increase PGM's quoting capacity and the accuracy of those quotes. Rather than making each quote a unique process produced on an individual basis (as had been their habitual approach), a systemic approach with standards and formal criteria was established for deciding whether or not to quote at all.

An additional challenge for PGM was to develop a rationale for balancing (1) flexibility and effectiveness (doing the right job) and (2) efficiency (getting the job done right). A key component in accomplishing these dual aims was developing a philosophy of cooperation throughout the company. This in turn was made possible when people were helped to see the organization as a system of links between and among processes, with each process designed to fulfill the needs underlying the vision and mission of the organization. Processes were viewed as end-to-end: everything possible was done to deliver quality products and services to the customer. From this vantage point, it is easy to see that the only way PGM could succeed was to act in accordance with the values of cooperation and teamwork. In a continuous improvement culture, all employees should understand their own contribution to the aims of the organization. Everyone at all levels of PGM needed to work together to improve processes and systems that served customers — both external and internal. In addition, end-to-end processes were necessary for the most efficient operations to support the production of quality products and the provision of quality services — a dream very dear to Hockenberger's heart.

Human Resource Development

At PGM, the human resource development ART explored the concept of a permanent versus a temporary labor force. It hoped to reduce layoffs and, if possible, eliminate them. We helped the team to examine the core competencies that PGM needed and to identify people who had related capabilities. The team could then consider this "core group" concept when developing policies for advancement and planning management succession.

Training and developing people to help them reach their fullest potential—for themselves as well as for the company—became an important value. Numerous training needs were identified, including learning to work together as self-directed team members and how to deal with confrontation and collusion. PGM determined that all employees would be given opportunities for personal development through such efforts as cross-training and continuing education. In addition, PGM increased feedback on employee performance and placed more emphasis on recognizing the whole person. Other training efforts involved the more experienced employees teaching their expertise to new employees.

Internal communication lines also opened and expanded. A centralized, integrated data base was designed to maintain company records. The company newsletter published not only reports on quality and delivery and news about employee benefits but also information about expansion programs and visiting customers. Top managers shared what they were learning in workshops and seminars. And more personal items appeared, such as employee birthdays and employment anniversaries, announcements of sports tournaments and parties, and word games and recipes. These communications helped emphasize the human side of enterprise.

Moving Toward Continuous Improvement

There are two main issues in implementing a continuous improvement culture, and both were encountered at PGM. One concerns the desire to implement continuous improvement; the other concerns the systems required to support that desire. With respect to the desire, continuous improvement must be an intrinsic value of the organization if people are to engage in the process. For openness and quality to be effective organizational strategies, people must be intrinsically motivated to improve the system and its products and services. World-class competition requires loyal, whole-hearted commitment and superior competence on the part of each person and each group.

This intrinsic motivation springs from several sources:

- A belief in and commitment to the organization's purpose and aims
- Management and leadership behaviors and processes that empower people to embrace continuous improvement
- Support for accomplishment, including time, tools, and other resources
- Systems that enable people to take pride in their accomplishments

Doing the Right Things Right

While openness and quality set the direction for the organization, continuous improvement provides the best way of closing gaps between current and ideal performance. If strategic direction involves doing the right things, then continuous improvement involves doing things right. The combination of a clear strategic direction and continuous improvement therefore involves both effectiveness and efficiency — doing the right things right. To sustain the organization's capacity to match products and services to customer needs, the system of improvement must include:

- A process for gathering data from customers
- A process for planning activities to improve performance and quality
- Methods for developing and carrying out improvements

The central focus of learning in an organization is meeting customer needs. Matching products and services with customer needs depends upon the interaction of three variables:

1. Systems — all people serve customers through systems.
2. Variation — all systems are affected by variation.
3. People — people can manage and reduce system variation.

People who are planning continuous improvement activities or who are involved in carrying out such activities need to visualize work as a process and the organization as a system of linked processes (Moen and Nolan, 1987). All people at all levels of the organization must be involved in implementing the strategies of openness and quality. Action research and continuous improvement are essential prerequisites for sustainable high performance. The Plan-Do-Check-Act cycle is used by all employees as they pursue the challenge of matching products and services with customer needs over time.

For learning and continuous improvement to become the modus operandi of the organization, the right information must get to the right person at the right time to facilitate decision making. That requires an integration of business performance management systems and other kinds of data management tools. At the macro level, it involves the integration of marketing, operations, human resources, and financial subsystems. At the micro level, it requires that people be equipped to use the basic tools of quality improvement, including flowcharting, Pareto analysis, control charts, statistical methods, and planned experiments. Finally, continuous improvement requires a change in the behavior of each individual, which together constitutes cultural change for the organization as a whole.

Leadership for Continuous Improvement

For a successful change process to occur, top leadership must provide a supportive environment and encourage experimentation, which means giving people opportunities to be creatively involved in process improvement activities. It also means that any existing barriers and constraints in the organization must be identified and removed or modified so that associated negative experiences are also removed or reduced. Senior management must both lead and exemplify the changes they seek in the organization. In other words, they must "walk the talk."

The role of leadership in enabling continuous improvement is not merely to provide resources, as important as that is. Perhaps even more important is leadership's ability to:

- Create disequilibrium through dissatisfaction with the current state,
- Provide a vision of a better future,
- Provide a plan for closing the gap between the current and future states, and
- Model continuous improvement and learning.

Without such leadership, in place of learning there will be decay.

Evaluating Results and Making Adaptations

Even though PGM had other ARTs functioning, the company focused its early efforts primarily on marketing and human resource development. This choice was made to strengthen the company's position in the short term by retaining current customers and recruiting and retaining new customers. Thus customer retention was the strategic focus of our short-term efforts. Table 4.2 displays some milestones and indicators PGM used as it took action in marketing and human resource development.

The diagnostic review process outlined in Chapter Three helped PGM's leaders examine their goals in terms of where the company was at the time, where they wanted to be, how they were going to get there, who was "going to drive," who was going to "pay for the trip," and how they would know when they had arrived. We therefore had built the evaluation process into the diagnostic phase.

Summary

When we started working with PGM, it was enmeshed in maintaining the status quo and reacting to crises rather than focused on a vision and planning ahead. The innovation and creativity that once characterized the company had become superseded by a need for stability and consistency. PGM was not learning from its experiences; it was losing its customer base, and departments were blaming one another for the loss.

Table 4.2. PGM's Milestones and Indicators
in Marketing and Human Resource Development.

	Milestone or Indicator	Timeline
Marketing	Hire marketing consultant to write marketing plan.	1-2 months
	Develop mission statement and marketing goals.	2 months
	Assess market potential of firm's products in various geographical regions.	3 months
	Develop strategies and tactics to meet management's goals.	4 months
	Write the plan and present it to management.	4-5 months
Human resource development	Hire human resource consultant to design and specify a system to put in place.	1-2 months
	Implement the specified system. Ensure it is fully integrated with PGM's management team.	2-3 months
	Prepare a report outlining the results of instituting a high-performance organization. Submit report to management.	4-6 month

Our principal tasks were to move PGM from a reactive mindset to a more strategic-creative mindset and to restore the company's original team-focused culture. We began by taking the executives through a strategic planning process and helping them establish a collaborative, team-oriented culture. This new culture employed Action Research Teams for marketing, bidding and finances, the engineering-manufacturing interface, and human resources. In Chapter Five, we examine how the Open Organization Model relates to PGM.

FIVE

LINKING EXEMPLARY CUSTOMER SERVICE TO VALUES AND RELATIONSHIPS

In Chapter Four, we discussed the case of Precision Grinding and Manufacturing (PGM), an organization that had lost contact with its customers and was therefore no longer meeting their needs. Because PGM's "presenting problem" (the original problem we were hired to address) was customer service (or contribution), our point of entry into the organization was through window nine of the Open Organization Model (see Figure 5.1).

Because an organization's ability to deliver quality service is a function of its unity and its internal and external responsiveness at every level, our work requires an examination of individuals and groups and the organization as a whole. A company's values, vision, mission, and goals must align, as well as its operations and processes, its routines and rewards. The common aim of all activities in the open organization is to support the ongoing matching of products and services to the customers' needs. Customers follow from needs, and potential customers are anyone who has the need.

Applying the Model to the Case of PGM

An organization's mission statement should therefore reflect the needs that it intends to satisfy. PGM's mission was to be a high-

Figure 5.1. Contribution in the Open Organization Model.

	Unity	Internal responsiveness	External responsiveness
Individual	1 Values	2 Congruence	3 Connection
Group	4 Shared purpose	5 Quality relationships	6 Collaboration
Organization	7 Shared vision	8 Alignment	**9 Contribution**

performing organization that did a good job of meeting and exceeding its customers' expectations. It wanted to continue to take on the most difficult tooling and manufacturing problems while maintaining its international reputation for quality work. To do that, the organization needed to strengthen its commitment to its customers. To work through its problems, PGM had to have a solid grasp of customer service. PGM had three very obvious problems in this regard:

1. It did not know who its customers were, and did not know its customers' needs and requirements (window nine).
2. There was very little alignment of systems around PGM's mission of providing excellent products and services to its customers (window eight).
3. It had no clear vision that extolled the value and centrality of the customers (window seven).

The difference between the winners and losers in today's business environment is often very subtle. It most often hinges on a company's ability to deliver service faster and better than its competitors. The Open Organization Model hypothesizes that an organization's ability to deliver quality service is a function of unity, internal responsiveness, and external responsiveness, as we saw in Chapter Two.

Unity — effective organizations work hard to achieve a high degree of alignment between purpose and process. Unity involves three aspects:

- Alignment of vision, values, and goals
- Alignment of operations and processes
- Alignment of routines and rewards

Internal responsiveness — effective organizations gather and use data from their internal environment to align and coordinate the systems and processes required to deliver quality services.

External responsiveness — effective organizations learn how to gather and effectively use data from customers, suppliers, and other stakeholders in the community.

The Essentials of Customer Service

As previously indicated, PGM had lost sight of its customers. In other words, its external responsiveness (window nine) was low; as a result, it was providing products that failed to meet customer needs and did not have competitive prices. Therefore, one of our first interventions was to find out what customers thought and felt about PGM and its products and services.

Evaluating Customer Service

The quality of service is more difficult to evaluate than the quality of goods. Still, the literature on service quality reveals several themes that influence how customers view quality.

Theme 1. Customers define the criteria for service quality. Because service is an intangible, customers have more difficulty evaluating services than goods; services therefore tend to be more difficult to market.

Theme 2. Customers evaluate service in terms of both outcome and process. When you get your car serviced, you evaluate the experience in terms of how well the car works and how easy it was for you to deal with the customer service representative. For instance, you might avoid a particular service department, despite it being more convenient, simply because the service representative was discourteous to you.

Theme 3. The only judgments that count in evaluating service quality are those defined by the customer. You can assess the quality of a product (tangible) with your mind, but you judge the quality of a service (intangible) by your perceptions and your heart. The service department manager where you took your car might never understand that it was not the quality of the repairs that led you to switch to the dealer on the other side of town; it was the way you were spoken to, the amount of time you had to wait, and the employees' unwillingness to respond to your specific needs. Specifically, service quality is judged by how well a provider performs in relation to a customer's expectations. The key to ensuring quality service is to meet or exceed customer expectations.

The most significant distinction between goods and services is that goods yield *possessions* while services yield *experiences*. With a service, production and consumption happen simultaneously. The quality of the service is therefore a function of the interaction between the customer and the customer's contact. Because the customer's attitudes, recent experiences, style of relating to others, and ability to communicate all impact the service provider, the customer becomes a very active participant in the production of services.

Criteria Used to Evaluate Provider-Customer Interactions

Several years ago a major utility consortium asked us to investigate how its customers evaluated service — an important concern for this particular company. It had requested a rate increase to finance construction of a nuclear power plant, and it was asked to provide a rationale as to why it should be allowed to raise rates. Using a focus group methodology, we asked customers to describe two experiences: one when they felt they had received exemplary service from the utility company and one when they believed they had received poor service. We then asked them what made the service good or poor.

The interviews helped us define several attributes that customers always associated with quality service; these attributes include:

- Competence
- Trustworthiness
- Timeliness
- Personal concern for the customer
- Willingness to listen to the customer
- Treating the customer as important
- Ability to understand the customer

Zeithaml, Parasuraman, and Berry (1990) used a similar methodology to uncover what appear to be the core criteria by which customers evaluate the service provided by an organization and decide whether to continue using that company's services. These criteria are listed and defined in Table 5.1.

We have developed a survey using the preceding dimensions of service. (See the description of the Customer Satisfaction Survey in Resource C.) Studies in which we have asked customers, as well as providers, to rate the most important of these criteria have consistently shown that, for current customers, reliability and responsiveness are the most important features of service, while tangibles is the least. Providers rate tangibles as most important and responsiveness as least. Evidently, it is all too easy for providers to be out of tune with their customers.

By asking customers what they thought about PGM, we learned that the organization was not responding to customer requests for cost-effective products; therefore, those customers were finding alternative means of meeting their needs.

Improving Responsiveness to Customers

To create a more responsive organization, it was necessary for PGM to develop a vision and value system in which customers were the center of all activity (window seven). To do so, the

Table 5.1. Key Criteria by Which Customers Judge Quality.

Criteria and Definition	Illustrations
Tangibles — appearance of physical facilities, equipment, personnel, communication materials	Are the facilities attractive? Are customer service reps dressed nicely? Do customer service reps speak pleasantly? Do the tools used by the repair reps look modern?
Reliability — ability to perform the promised service dependably and accurately	Do people call me back when promised? Is my statement free of errors? Is my bill correct?
Responsiveness — willingness to help customers and provide prompt service	When I have a problem, is it resolved quickly? Does the company treat my problem as unique? Is the customer service rep willing to give me a specific time when someone will arrive for installation or repairs?
Assurance — credibility: trustworthiness, believability, honesty of service provider	Are my transactions processed without fumbling around? Can the providers perform the tasks they are expected to perform? Does the company have a good reputation? Do sales reps refrain from pressuring me to buy? Am I told the truth about my rates?
Empathy — understanding and caring for the customer and his or her unique needs	Am I recognized as a customer? Does the sales rep know my goals? Can the customer service rep explain the fees I am expected to pay? Are the customer service reps willing to listen to me? Is it easy for me to talk to the firm's representative?

Source: Adapted from Zeithaml, Parasuraman, and Berry (1990). Reprinted with the permission of The Free Press, Macmillan Publishing Company, a Member of Paramount Publishing from *Delivering Quality Service: Balancing Customer Perceptions and Expectations* by Valarie A. Zeithaml, A. Parasuraman, and Leonard L. Berry. Copyright © 1990 by The Free Press.

organization had to be aligned around these core values (window eight).

One reason why PGM was not price competitive was that the engineering group focused more on the product than on the customer. They really valued doing high-quality work. In the process, however, they began to lose sight of the customer. When

PGM's engineering group emphasized higher and higher product standards, individual engineers and machinists began placing more value on the design and machining of the product than on their relationship with the customer. These new production standards increased the company's costs so much that it could no longer be competitive in the marketplace. As a result, it lost customers.

Our second level of intervention dealt specifically with the lack of internal responsiveness and alignment among the various departments (window eight). As we mentioned in Chapter Four, PGM's reorganization had created conditions for internal conflict and competition, and employee morale had plummeted because of layoffs and reorganization. The strategic team development activity, as well as the formation of ARTs in finance, human resources, manufacturing and engineering, and marketing, was undertaken to help create the needed alignment within and between the various functions.

Finally, we had to intervene at the level of the individual. When we arrived at PGM, it did not have a trusting climate. Individual managers were behaving as if other managers and employees were not competent. People were torn between their dreams and their need for security. There was very little leeway for taking risks. An attitude pervaded that employees could not afford to make any mistakes. When employees entered unknown territory, fear and nervousness pervaded. They tended to let attention to detail take precedence.

There was not much employee recognition, and what little there was emphasized being "perfect." Many employees felt they had to "practically live at work to be successful." Experience was highly valued and guided learning. Old toolmakers were truly valued; young toolmakers were not.

PGM tended to quote all prospective jobs the same way, regardless of their type, size, or importance. A fear of misquoting tended to limit innovative risk taking and encouraged a conservative manufacturing approach. This fear also led to excessive sign-offs and approvals, which did nothing to build an atmosphere of trust. Employees behaved as if they believed customers were trying to take advantage of them. An excess of qualifiers, requests for changes, and statements like "pending engineering review" gave customers the impression that PGM would take their jobs only if certain terms were met.

An obvious challenge for PGM was to satisfy quality requirements and still keep costs down. But organizations cannot build good relationships with their customers when their own employees are not feeling good about themselves. When people are really worried about their own welfare, they let clients and customers fall through the cracks. That is essentially what happened at PGM, and these individual concerns bring us back to window one.

Interconnections in the Open Organization Model

Using the Open Organization Model becomes progressive. If you are fairly certain individuals are on board and are doing okay, then you need to make certain that groups are on board too. Then you need to monitor the organization as a whole.

At the individual level for PGM, clarifying values (window one) strengthened personal congruence (window two) so individuals could connect with their customers (window three). This connection had a direct impact on service.

At the group level, each ART developed a shared purpose (window four). Open communications strengthened relationships (window five), and collaborative efforts (window six) led directly to improved performance.

At the organization level, the development of a shared vision (window seven) by the executive team established vision (window seven), strengthened alignment (window eight), and finally led to improved service (window nine).

Although the point of entry into PGM was window nine, we began our work with executive team development (window seven) in order to reestablish clear focus (vision, mission, and goals) for the desired future state and to clarify and reach consensus on values. This focus helped build cohesiveness and restore commitment within the executive team. Once we built rapport and got the executive team on board, we started our diagnostic activities. We conducted an opinion survey to determine where the organization's problems were so they could be corrected.

We worked with key individuals to identify core competencies and to establish a permanent work force. An example of a core competency at PGM was being able to convert an often inaccurate engineering drawing of a part submitted by a customer into a working drawing a machinist could use to produce some prototype parts. Determining the cost of making the prototype would then help in making an accurate bid. When the customer drawings were not accurate enough to formulate a good bid, much time had to be invested in interacting with the customer to determine what the customer wanted the product to do, what the customer's quality standards were, and so on. In PGM's case, the loss of customer contact was particularly important. Employees who were focused on concerns about job security did not always put adequate effort into producing a sound bid, and they were not willing to invest enough time with their customers to get them involved with the design and the application of the prototype part. This process often led to incorrect estimates, and subsequently, to marginal profits and sometimes substantial losses. We found that when PGM's leaders and employees were able to align values with policies and operational procedures with a customer focus, they could develop the kinds of standards and practices that would enable them to succeed. The bottom line: PGM is alive and well today.

Summary

At Precision Grinding and Manufacturing, the presenting problem was an inability to respond to customer needs and requirements. The company was losing customers, and its very survival was threatened. In attempting to resolve this problem, diagnosis using the Open Organization Model revealed that low responsiveness to customers began with differences in the personal values of the company's senior leaders. A service problem at the organization level (window nine) had been influenced by individual conflicts over what was important and worth striving for, and how to organize for success.

Only after these personal value conflicts were identified

and articulated was it apparent that PGM's reorganization along functional lines (which was motivated by individual needs for status and power) led to a decline in the company's ability to respond to its customers. The resolution of these differences led to the reevaluation of PGM's organization and a subsequent reorganization back to the original project team model. This refocusing helped the company to develop practices that enabled its employees to meet customer needs in a cost-effective, intelligent manner.

SIX

BUILDING OPEN GROUPS: THE CASE OF THE TRAVELERS INSURANCE COMPANY

When we labor for outcomes in our organizations, we often spend many hours huddled with two or more associates — a group of colleagues. We gripe, celebrate, mourn, or problem solve. Relationships in organizations can function at many levels: person to person, person to group, person to organization, group to group, and group to organization. The dynamics of groups at work become a crucial part of our organizational existence. Understanding how groups function and how to increase their effectiveness is key to both personal and organizational success. As problems become more complex, group performance becomes even more critical to business success. The case study in Chapters Six and Seven describes an intervention from the level of the group at The Travelers Insurance Company, Managed Care and Employee Benefits Operations (MCEBO).

Some Historical Perspective

Managed Care and Employee Benefits Operations (MCEBO), a twelve-thousand-person division of The Travelers Insurance Company, was facing a challenge. The division had just had a year of reduced profits caused in large part by a rapidly changing

83

marketplace and fueled by ever-increasing state and federal health-care regulations. In addition to the company's financial and marketplace difficulties, the division president had just retired, and the company president, Dick Booth, was acting as a transitional leader while actively searching for a new leader to run MCEBO.

One of Booth's first actions was to establish eight "Change Leadership Teams," which were charged with the task of identifying profit opportunities. These teams operated like the Action Research Teams we described in Chapter Three. Their task required a twofold approach:

1. The groups had to identify more clearly their customers and understand their needs and requirements.
2. They had to redesign and/or enhance products to better meet the identified customer needs.

Each team addressed a separate business issue:

*   Compensation Strategy Team — to develop compensation programs that would support increased profitability and revenue growth.
*   Profit Expansion Team — to identify actions that would lead to an improvement in profit and revenue growth.
*   Profit Enhancement Team — to improve near-term profitability in particular market segments.
*   Managed Care Strategy Development Team — to identify how managed care investments would be managed and prioritized, to identify the geographic and product areas that MCEBO would focus on over time to serve particular accounts, and then to determine the near-term actions that would ensure an appropriate marketing and profit focus.
*   Claim Payout and Cost Reduction Team — to formulate and execute a series of initiatives that would reengineer, streamline, and simplify claim operations and customer service functions, with an eye toward enhancing customer service.
*   Home Office/Corporate Expense Reductions Team — to eliminate nonessential activities and expenditures by ensur-

ing proper allocation of resources; to support the profit/service plans established by the Change Leadership Teams.

* Product Profitability Enhancement Team — to make significant strides in developing modular and automated products that would be easy for MCEBO customers to use and that could be sold aggressively by the field sales staff; to improve MCEBO employees' understanding of the key profit levers in each major product.

* Change Management Team (CMT) — to focus on managing the changes that would result from the work of the other teams, fulfilling the work of a Transformation Leadership Team, guiding the overall effort. This team was charged with developing and implementing a program to promote productive change at all levels of MCEBO and to ensure that senior management's actions and communications reinforced a clear sense of direction.

The Change Management Team, led by Dan Plunkett, an internal organizational development consultant, comprised both line and staff members from across The Travelers. The eight members of the team were chosen by Dick Booth. Its members included some of the brightest, most highly skilled and informed people in MCEBO and across the corporation. Special consideration was given to those employees who had demonstrated a willingness to drive change and confront organizational problems openly.

Discovering the Problem

An initial task of the Change Management Team was to evaluate the division using a force field analysis technique. Force field analysis views an organization in terms of a dynamic balance of opposing forces within that organization's social-psychological space. Kurt Lewin (1951) calls these forces "driving" and "restraining" forces (see Figure 6.1).

Driving forces initiate change and keep it moving. Restraining forces work against any shift in equilibrium. When an imbalance develops between driving and restraining forces,

Figure 6.1. Driving and Restraining Forces.

Restraining forces: inhibiting change

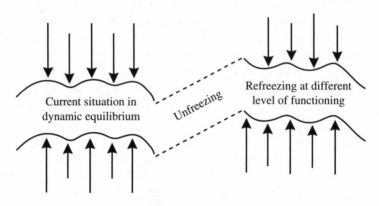

Driving forces: pushing for change

Source: Mink, Esterhuysen, Mink, and Owen, 1993.

it stimulates disequilibrium, which acts as a catalyst for change. Because large organizations often have mechanisms in place that ensure their stability and dampen efforts for change, oftentimes disequilibrium must be introduced deliberately to "unfreeze" these mechanisms.

In the unfreezing process, functional relationships are broken and habitual patterns of interaction are abandoned. The challenge to learn is introduced. While an organization is going through the unfreezing process, it must experiment with new forms or configurations. Experimentation, of course, goes hand in hand with risk. Therefore, people must feel released from any constraints related to learning, problem solving, and risk taking. They must break free of anything that inhibits productive effort. For transformative change and innovation, leaders must create an environment that encourages people to take risks to make needed improvements.

Lewin's model of force field analysis suggests how to initiate change in a system by shifting the emphasis or impact of the driving and restraining forces. Once a change occurs at a new level, forces must "refreeze," or restabilize, the system, or the change is likely to be temporary because as soon as the press for change is diminished or a constraint against the change is reintroduced, individuals who have not yet internalized the change may revert to their previous habits. Force field analysis helps team members identify the personal, group, organizational, and other forces that push toward change and those that inhibit change. Force field analysis also provides a framework to assist the analysis and evaluation of forces so that a team can make decisions on change strategy.

Determining a Strategy

The results of the force field analysis at MCEBO suggested that the underlying problem was a closedness that disempowered MCEBO's people. To change this situation, Plunkett proposed an organizational change process based on open systems theory, the Open Organization Model, and the Total Transformation Management Process, or TTMP (Mink, Esterhuysen, Mink, and Owen, 1993). Quite briefly, the TTMP involves the steps shown in Figure 6.2.

This process incorporates the nine windows of Open Organization Model during the intervention phase. It also embraces action research. The outer ring in Figure 6.2 and its inward-pointing arrows represent the ongoing probing and reflection that take place through action research.

This change process, which MCEBO adopted as the MCEBO Change Process (MCP), was presented to Dick Booth, and after considerable discussion on the details of each step, he agreed to use it to address the issues the division was facing.

Evaluating the Need for Change and
Determining the Future and Present States

Once the Change Leadership Teams had been formed, MCEBO's next steps focused on clarifying the need for the changes, determining the forces and resources required to execute the changes and, most importantly, examining and understanding the current

Figure 6.2. The Total Transformation Management Process (TTMP).

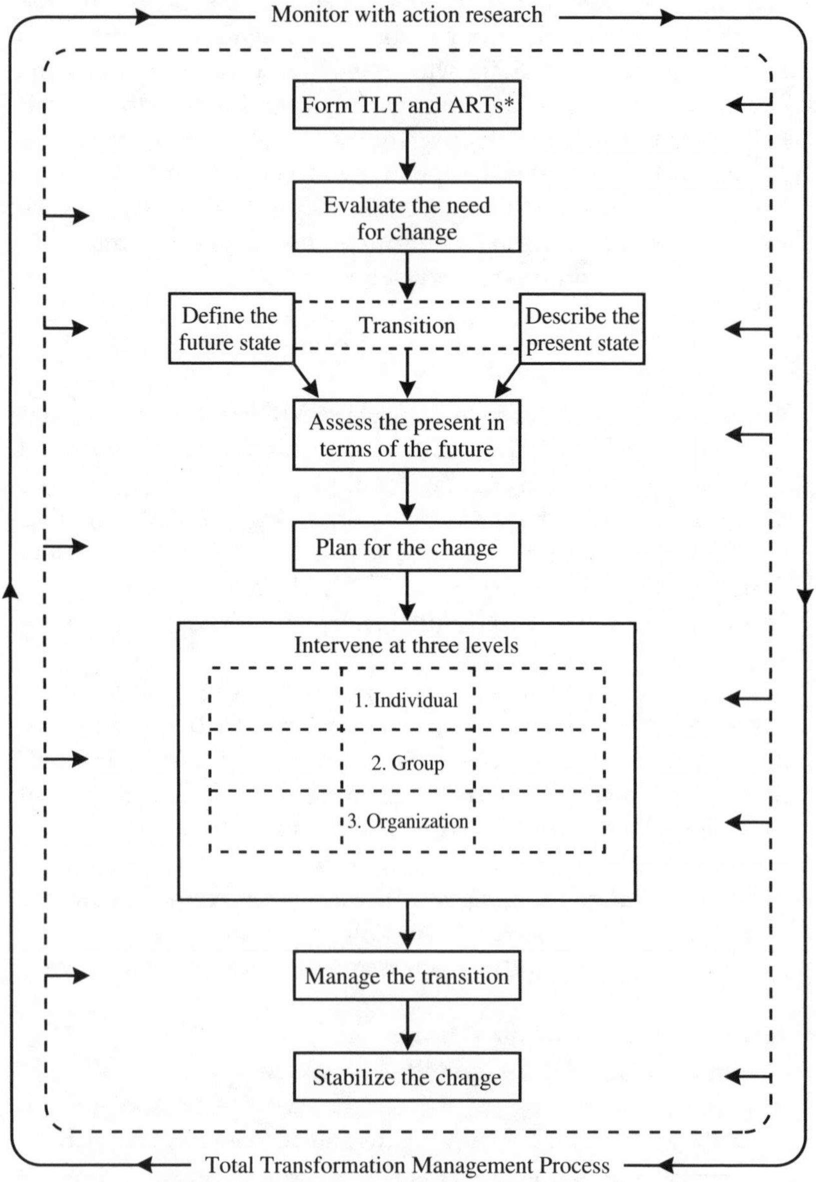

*TLT = Transformation Leadership Team
ART = Action Research Team

Source: Mink, Esterhuysen, Mink, and Owen, 1993.

organizational climate of the division. To accomplish these steps and to define the present state, the Open Organization Profile (OOP) was administered to the division's top two tiers. This ninety-item survey (described in Resource C) measures the relative openness of the organization and provides data pertaining to each of the nine windows of the Open Organization Model. It helps users understand, in their own words, where the significant barriers to organizational change might reside.

Booth then announced that Elliot Gerson, the senior vice president of financial services for The Travelers, would head MCEBO and that Booth would remain involved for the transition period. At the same time, structural and personnel reorganizations were announced throughout the division.

During the early days of Gerson's tenure, Dan Plunkett, under the auspices of the Change Management Team, familiarized Gerson with the MCEBO Change Process. Gerson had earned a reputation for being action oriented and had produced dramatic changes and improved profits in the organizations he had previously led. Plunkett positioned the Open Organization Profile as a tool that had captured information about MCEBO that could prove invaluable in improving the organization's effectiveness, thereby contributing to the achievement of its aggressive goals.

Gerson's support for the MCEBO Change Process was strong and public. He announced openly that if the process had not already been in place, he would have instituted a similar process on his own. As the new leader, Gerson was already aware that MCEBO had some significant problems, and he knew that rapid improvement was expected. One of his top priorities was to create an organization based on trust, honesty, candor, and open communication. He believed that only within this type of organization would MCEBO people accomplish the dramatic turnaround that was needed.

To determine how effectively the division was operating, the Change Management Team administered the Open Organization Profile to the management team members and their direct reports. (Although a broader sample would have been preferable, the scope was limited because of time constraints.)

Participants rated themselves, their teams, and all of

MCEBO in areas such as degree of unity and alignment around shared purposes, planning and problem solving, team development and goal clarity, cooperation with others, and MCEBO's ability to adapt to marketplace changes. The assessment was conducted to identify issues of nonperformance and to determine how deficiencies affected the company's performance.

Plunkett shared the results of the assessment with Gerson and Booth, along with recommendations from the Change Management Team to follow through on the next steps of the MCEBO Change Process. The results of the survey reiterated and specified in more actionable detail those issues identified earlier by the force field analysis:

1. Management was generally distrusted and viewed as distant and removed from employees and the business.
2. Although development and good performance occurred within specific teams in MCEBO, there was little cooperation across teams.
3. Decisions were not made at the right levels, and true delegation of authority was limited.
4. Management did not hold itself accountable enough for its results.
5. Business results were suffering because of a lack of direction, cooperation, accountability, and employee confidence.
6. The organization was characterized by fear, dependence, deference to power and authority, formality, aversion to confrontation and risk taking, and a pervasive sense of entitlement. Many people feared retribution if they took a risk and did not succeed.

The same month, the specific recommendations of the other Change Leadership Teams were announced. As expected, the recommended changes regarding MCEBO's business methods were bold and dramatic. For example, it was recommended that products be totally repositioned in the marketplace, that the sales and service work force be reorganized nationwide, and that most key functions be realigned. The announcement of these recommendations provided additional momentum for the MCEBO Change Process because senior management recognized that significant change would be difficult within the existing organization.

Assessing the Present in Terms of the Future and Planning for Change

To contrast the present state with the future vision and to plan the changes that would help fulfill that vision, the findings of the Open Organization Profile were discussed at Gerson's first off-site session with his new direct reports. Many of the senior management team members had been appointed only days earlier, together with the announcement of the Change Leadership Teams' recommendations.

At this session, facilitated by Plunkett, Booth participated as a co-leader with Gerson. Gerson and Booth encouraged ownership and responsibility on the Change Management Team for the findings of the Open Organization Profile. Gerson and Booth's statements confirmed the group's overwhelming feeling that there was no higher priority for the success of the business than to address the diagnosed problems with openness, courage, and determination.

In keeping with the goals of developing more openness and honesty, the tier one managers (those on the Change Management Team) agreed to share the findings with tier two employees (their direct reports). They also agreed that Plunkett should facilitate the feedback sessions to ensure that tier two members addressed the issues identified through the Open Organization Profile.

The Change Management Team was then dissolved, and responsibility for implementation of the change process was assigned to the senior management team, with Gerson and Booth taking ultimate responsibility.

Applying the Strategy

Consistent with a participative action research model, Gerson and Booth decided to use a highly participative problem-solving format when feeding back data to tier two employees. This decision was based partly on the findings of the Open Organization Profile, which indicated that tier two employees did not feel involved in organizational decision making, and that there was a lack of trust among the top two tiers of the division. Thus, the problem-solving format not only fed back data to assist in planning actions for intervention at individual, group, and organization levels, it was itself an action to address some problem areas.

Before the tier two feedback sessions, Gerson sent a personal message to each participant emphasizing the importance of the meetings and making clear his expectation that participants be frank and bold in their recommendations for improvement. He also assured participants that he would tolerate no negative repercussions for honest participation during these sessions.

Plunkett facilitated three off-site sessions, with groups of twenty-five tier two members attending each session. The groups were cross-functional and randomly sorted. Using the findings of the Open Organization Profile, each group defined critical problem areas, identified root causes, and recommended solutions. Each group selected a representative to help consolidate the work of all groups.

The tier two representatives identified five critical problem areas and recommended solutions to the senior management team. A common theme that emerged from these five problem areas was a lack of trust toward and among MCEBO management.

Many of the small groups during the tier two problem-solving sessions had identified past leadership style (being confrontational, inconsistent, theoretical, and control oriented) as a root cause of some of the trust issues that had emerged. Lack of trust was communicated clearly in the first critical problem presented to the senior management team: "MCEBO culture is an environment lacking in openness, trust, and honesty." This problem alone accounted for almost half of the discussion time during the meeting. Trust was also the area where real change would take the most time. Intellectually, all of the people involved seemed to believe that the MCEBO's organization should be based on openness, trust, and honesty (including open disagreement and confrontation); but the lessons of the former organization ran deep, and many were still unwilling to risk their careers to make the needed changes.

Intervening and Monitoring Change

The senior management team committed themselves to reviewing the recommendations and to informing all tier two employees about which would be implemented and which would not, as well as the thought process behind those decisions. Gerson and Booth both publicly declared their commitment to constant, meaningful communication as the critical element in building trust and creating a climate of openness and honesty. They believed this climate to be prequisite to accomplishing business objectives.

The senior management team then met with tier two members to discuss the actions that would be taken and to address the critical problem areas identified by those members during their discussion of organizational effectiveness. These actions ran the gamut from the clearly measurable and easily accomplished ("publish a MCEBO organization summary") to more challenging, long-term promises ("be responsible for enhancing communication in our own departments" and "promote effective cross-functional teams").

During this meeting, the senior management team, led by Gerson and Booth, modeled the openness, honesty, and candor they had been espousing. They posed numerous questions to the tier two members and continuously checked that they were accurately interpreting the work of tier two problem-solving groups. Tier two members, on the other hand, seemed somewhat hesitant to take significant risks within the open forum. They were much less vocal than might have been expected, based on their attitude and actions during and following the problem-solving sessions. Gerson encouraged everyone to take ownership and be accountable for fixing what was wrong with MCEBO. He reminded people that the entire organization had created the situation it was currently facing and that all of its members would need to be committed to improving its performance.

The results of the meeting were specific, agreed-upon actions, which were incorporated into each manager's performance evaluation standards:

1. Attend each other's staff meetings.
2. Hold skip-level meetings twice a month (where managers meet with members two levels below them in the organization to learn how things are going).
3. Complete annual performance reviews for direct reports and keep them updated.
4. Share the outcome of senior management team meetings with staff.
5. Involve staff (especially in the field) in decisions when appropriate.
6. Report business results clearly and regularly.
7. Develop and implement a communication strategy.
8. Follow through on implementation of the operations management review process and maintain accurate performance data.

Supervising managers evaluated performance against these standards every quarter. Gerson personally evaluated each member of the senior management team to make certain they were following through on their commitments.

At Gerson's request, Plunkett continued to play an active role in organizational effectiveness improvement efforts. The internal consulting staff reporting to Plunkett, all of whom have master's or doctoral degrees in organization development, education, or business administration, worked closely with various areas in the division to ensure that all agreed-upon actions were implemented. Plunkett took on the role of "conscience of the organization," monitoring activity to verify that change was really happening, that the senior managers were following through on their promises, and that the rest of the organization was upholding its end of the bargain.

Managing the Transition and Stabilizing the Change

At the beginning of the change implementation process, both Gerson and Booth insisted on reassessing the organization as a means of managing the transition and stabilizing the improvements. Periodic reassessments, using the Open Organization Profile, were therefore performed. Eight months into the implementation, assessments conducted by Plunkett indicated that the primary concerns of low trust and lack of cooperation had significantly improved. Dramatic flattening of the organization had occurred and important operating efficiencies had been accomplished. Almost forty million dollars in after-tax savings and over ten million dollars in nonsalary expenses had been achieved. The MCEBO Change Process had also produced a 55 percent increase in core earnings and a 16 percent increase in lives covered in managed health care networks such as health maintenance organizations.

Summary

Because MCEBO serves a marketplace that is in turmoil, it presents an especially challenging environment in which to achieve meaningful organizational change. Through the implementation of the MCEBO Change Process, the organization committed to using an open systems approach to maintain and improve its ability to respond effectively to a demanding, changing environment.

The underlying problem at MCEBO was a closed organization, in which people were distrustful, afraid, and disempowered. The organization undertook an extensive change management process, based on the Total Transformation Management Process, and took steps to enhance communication throughout the organization. Managers became more accessible and directly involved with employees, and a monitoring process was developed to provide ongoing support for a more trusting, open environment.

SEVEN

RENEWING TRUST AND QUALITY RELATIONSHIPS

The presenting problem at Managed Care and Employee Benefits Operations was quality relationships within the management team, so our point of entry into the organization was window five of the Open Organization Model (see Figure 7.1).

MCEBO's Five Critical Problem Areas

As indicated through the use of the participatory feedback of the results of the Open Organization Profile, the tier two representatives identified five critical problem areas. The people at MCEBO:

1. Felt they were not valued, trusted, or effectively involved in decision making;
2. Had low morale;
3. Felt that their work environment lacked openness, truth, and honesty;
4. Felt that communications were ineffective, inconsistent, and filled with mixed messages; and
5. Felt a lack of focus and organizational cooperation.

Figure 7.1. Quality Relationships in the Open Organization Model.

Unity	Internal responsiveness	External responsiveness
1 Values	2 Congruence	3 Connection
4 Shared purpose	5 **Quality relationships**	6 Collaboration
7 Shared vision	8 Alignment	9 Contribution

(Individual, Group, Organization label the three rows respectively.)

A common theme that emerged from these five areas was a lack of trust toward and among MCEBO management. Without a foundation of trust, it is impossible to develop quality relationships.

Building Truthful, Trusting Relationships

Trust is the state of readiness for unguarded interaction with someone or something. It has three determinants: the perception of competence, the perception of intentions, and the capacity for trusting (Tway, 1993; Tway and Davis, 1993). The *perception of competence* is our perception of the degree to which something or someone (including ourselves) is able to do what is needed and our perception of the degree of awareness, accuracy, and truth in representations of competence. The *perception of intentions* is our perception of a person's actions and the attribution that the actor's motives (including our own) are either self-serving or mutually serving, our perception of the degree to which there is a willingness to do what is needed, and our perception of the degree of awareness, accuracy, and truth in representations of intentions. The *capacity for trusting* appears first in our lives. Erik Erikson (1959) described this determinant as "an attitude toward oneself and the world derived from the experiences of the first year of life." Whether a child develops a basic sense of trust or of distrust depends on the quality of that child's maternal relationship (pp. 55–56, 63). According to MacGregor (1967, p. 163), trust is based on our perception of the other person rather than on that person's actions. We would add that our perceptions of the other person's intentions and competence determine our level of trust and that these perceptions are based on our capacity for trusting. (For an excellent examination of the role of perceptions in trust, see Garfinkel, 1963.)

Using the Model to Understand Underlying Causes

As the Open Organization Profile results and the follow-up feedback sessions demonstrated, many employees felt that they were not valued by MCEBO's senior management team. People wanted to be more involved and to receive feedback from management. Employees wanted management to demonstrate more commitment and responsiveness to their needs and concerns:
    An underlying cause was management's decision-making style. Because senior managers tended to make decisions without involving others, there was very little internal responsiveness to employee concerns (window five) and there was no alignment around a shared vision concerning empowerment and involvement (window seven). Employees wanted senior management to involve all levels in the decision-making process before making or announcing decisions. They wanted managers to:

- Support decision making at lower levels by acting to drive decisions to those levels;
- Redefine the role of product managers by empowering them with responsibility for the total product spectrum, including development, implementation, pricing, and profitability; and

- Reinforce decision-making responsibilities as part of each individual's job.

The Open Organization Model can help us understand the nature of the perceived problems and their solutions. As has been the case in previous chapters, we view the model as a heuristic tool that enables practitioners (managers, consultants, people who are assisting with organizational change) to diagnose a presenting problem correctly, discover valid strategies for dealing with the problem, and evaluate the results of those strategies.

The focus of this chapter is on window five — internal responsiveness at the group or team level, and the problems cited above are rooted in a lack of quality relationships. Thus here we discuss some prerequisites of effective teamwork and some issues regarding team dynamics that are pertinent when trying to introduce continuous improvement or other types of change into organizations. (See Mink, Mink, and Owen, 1987, and Mink, Esterhuysen, Mink, and Owen, 1993 for additional information on group development.)

Team Internal Responsiveness

Internal responsiveness at the group level suggests that the work team or unit has learned to appreciate and attend to its own needs and processes so that it is able to maintain itself while fulfilling its purposes. To accomplish this responsiveness, the team learns how to listen both to itself and to those in the environment in which it functions. Then it learns how to use this data to solve problems as they arise and to anticipate the future.

Internal responsiveness might also be viewed as the ability to make the right adaptation at the right time. An internally responsive team has boundaries in that it has a sense of its own identity. On the other hand, it is not so rigidly committed to this identity that it is unable to adjust and adapt to a changing environment. Instead, it is able to take in new data, analyze it in light of its mission, and make changes when required.

Characteristics of the Internally Responsive Team

How does an internally responsive team compare to an unresponsive team? Teams that are strong in internal responsiveness show higher levels of the following characteristics:

- Shared purpose
- Appreciation for and understanding of the context in which the team is functioning
- Level of communication
- Degree of commitment to team values and goals
- Level of empowerment of each individual on the team
- Level of evaluation of current versus expected performance
- Dedication to continuous improvement of processes and relationships
- Level of acceptance of individuals and their uniqueness
- Level of empathy or an appreciation and respect for each other
- Constructive level of openness
- Level of sharing of data, including feelings
- Degree of cohesiveness and interpersonal attraction
- Willingness to share power
- Level of empathy or an appreciation and respect for each other
- Number of opportunities for each individual to contribute and be recognized for her or his contribution
- Sense of belonging or connectedness to the team
- Number of efforts made to identify and solve problems
- Focus on tasks

One set of ideas that best seems to describe internally responsive teams is embedded in the same concepts used to describe quality relationships. According to the Open Organization Model, a group, team, or department within an organization cannot perform its tasks unless quality relationships are established within that team. Available research suggests that for long-term, sustained high performance, you must have quality relationships. A leader can coerce or persuade people to perform at their highest levels in the short term; in the long term, however, it will be impossible for the leader to sustain those levels of performance.

Many authors have attempted to describe a "quality relationship." However, Jack Gibb's (1978) definition still seems to provide one of the most succinct descriptions. According to Gibb, quality relationships are based on four growth processes:

1. Trusting — giving and receiving *acceptance*
2. Opening — giving and receiving *truth*
3. Realizing — giving and receiving *power*
4. Interbeing — giving and receiving *freedom*

Internally responsive teams seem to exhibit high levels of all four processes. The cultivation of trusting, opening, realizing, and interbeing enable a team to become productive; a balance of acceptance, truth, power, and freedom gives the team its strength.

Team Development and Teamwork

How do teams develop quality relationships? To develop a meaningful answer to this question, we have to appreciate the interconnectedness explicit in the nine windows of the open, adaptive organization. First, quality relationships are possible only when the people entering into the relationships are reasonably healthy. In other words, they must be:

*   Capable of entering and nurturing relationships that are based on trusting, opening, realizing, and interbeing;
*   Relatively free of the effects of the dysfunctional ways people are sometimes taught (although inadvertently) to relate to one another by parents; and
*   Open to learning and changing themselves.

Second, the organization must value and support the development of quality relationships. The organization provides the matrix in which team relationships unfold, just like the family typically provides the matrix in which individual development unfolds. When the organization models and encourages open, honest relationships, when it develops routines and rewards that encourage cooperation, it is possible for the team to develop the kinds of relationships required to become a high-performing team.

To better understand the effects of quality relationships on high performance, let us examine what is known about team development and teamwork. Teams come together for a specific purpose. Without a purpose there is no reason for a team to exist. Attainment of the shared purpose is the ultimate outcome of the team.

To enhance its chances of success, the group must deal with three underlying interpersonal issues:

1. Inclusion and acceptance
2. Control and giving and receiving influence
3. Self-esteem and individual and team productivity

In other words, for team members to develop commitment and become more productive, the team must provide an environment in which its members' deepest needs can be met. When the team enables individuals to meet their own needs for belonging, power, and competence, both individuals and the team prosper and succeed.

Table 7.1 addresses the ways in which commitment and productivity vary over time. As the table indicates, commitment and productivity wax and wane as issues of trust, acceptance, mutual influence, and problem solving are dealt with effectively and openly.

Considering this information, we reach two conclusions:

1. Quality interpersonal relationships within a group are essential to high performance.
2. There is a significant correlation between the quality of relationships in a team and that team's performance.

To focus on these conclusions, consider what a team must do to succeed. It must be able to:

Table 7.1. Developmental Stages of Productivity and Commitment.

Developmental Stage	Group Stage	Productivity Level	Commitment (Morale) Level
Developing trust	Orientation	Low	Moderate to high
Accepting and using individual differences	Dissatisfaction	Low to moderate	Low
Giving and receiving feedback	Resolution	Moderately high	Variable and improving
Solving problems	Production	High	High
Letting go and staying on task	Termination or resolution	Moderate to low	Moderate to low

- Collect and analyze data
- Understand causes and effects
- Solve problems
- Make plans
- Evaluate and choose between alternatives
- Provide mutual support
- Develop and evaluate strategies
- Uncover and manage conflicts
- Implement and manage plans
- Deal with setbacks
- Learn from experiences
- Keep on course
- Create and innovate
- Coordinate people and tasks

When we analyze this list of activities, three distinct categories emerge: task, maintenance, and individual. In other words, a team must perform those activities that enable it to accomplish its goals, maintain its integrity, and at the same time empower each team member to meet his or her needs for personal acceptance, social influence, power, and achievement, which results in enhanced self-esteem. When organized into these three categories, group activities can be viewed as shown in Table 7.2.

Table 7.2. Task, Maintenance, and
Individual Activities Required for Teamwork.

Activities	Description
Task	
Initiating	Get things going; keep things going by suggesting a structure or procedure, identifying a problem, or providing an idea
Seeking information and opinions	Ask for ideas, opinions, information, and data from others
Sharing information and opinions	Share relevant information, opinions, assumptions, suggestions, and concerns
Clarifying and elaborating	Clear up confusion, explain, give examples, identify issues, interpret events, build onto ideas
Summarizing	Pull things together, restate ideas, organize ideas
Consensus testing and evaluating	Check for clarity on decisions or solutions and ensure all have been heard and agree or disagree
Coordinating	Organize and provide structure, keep records, and plan for future sessions
Maintenance	
Encouraging	Provide warm, friendly responses and gestures
Managing conflict	Recognize, identify, and clarify differences of opinion, perceptions, and ideas; encourage listening and consideration of alternatives; value differences and look for creative options
Gate keeping	Manage communication flow and keep communications channels open; encourage others to participate; monitor participation
Diagnosing and facilitating group functioning	Identify and express group feelings, tone, issues, problems, and accomplishments, and make process suggestions
Listening actively and sharing feelings	Paraphrase, reflect feelings, encourage openness, share own feelings
Acknowledging others	Recognize and appreciate the contributions of team members and the team's accomplishments
Individual	
Opening up	Share relevant information and data that helps the group perform its tasks
Getting involved	Engage totally with the group and its work
Exhibiting mutuality	Develop collaborative relationships based on equality and mutual empowerment
Sharing influence	Exhibit power and intiative and remain open to others' initiatives

Each activity requires valid data and competence to complete successfully. What makes it possible for people to collaborate successfully, to attain the level of sharing required to manage all these activities? A significant part of the answer can be seen in the quality of the organizational climate in which the team operates. A positive climate and quality relationships can be characterized by some of the following norms and dimensions of good team performance:

- Shared purpose — team members are committed to common goals.
- High level of trust — people do what they say they are going to do and share relevant data.
- High level of respect for and full use of individual differences — people accept one another.
- High level of giving and receiving feedback — people relate as equals even though they differ in social power or position.
- High level of problem solving — the team and its members are very productive.
- High level of task focus — people keep on track and stay in the present.

The performance of a team can be assessed along the two levels shown in Table 7.1: (1) team member morale and commitment (a process variable) and (2) team productivity (an outcome variable). In our research on team effectiveness, we have found that high-performing teams differ from less effective teams in both process and outcome measures. First, they have quality relationships as measured by the level of morale and commitment. These teams typically exhibit high levels of trust, acceptance, feedback, problem solving, and focus. Second, they are more productive than teams with ineffective or dysfunctional relationships. The bottom line is that to function effectively a team must develop quality relationships.

Effective teams are characterized by a commitment to a common purpose. The shared purpose enables individual team members to identify with the team. It provides the energy or motivation to learn and work together; it provides a direction or target for all activities; it provides a backdrop for decision making and problem solving; and it provides a benchmark against which to judge performance. Shared purpose provides the unity that enables collective coordinated action. Through shared effort toward a shared goal, synergy becomes possible.

Team External Responsiveness

Even with shared purpose (unity) and quality relationships (internal responsiveness), however, a team is not whole because it does not exist in a vacuum. It is part of a larger set of relationships — those between itself and its suppliers and customers. As we have already said, a team's purpose can always be defined in terms of satisfying customer needs, be they internal or external. In the absence of the ability and the will to talk with suppliers and customers (external responsiveness), the team does not have the data it requires to fulfill its purpose. This data closes the circle, so to speak. It tells the team what it is to accomplish (meet a need) and for whom (customers). It tells the team what is needed (input and resources) and from whom (suppliers) to meet the customers' needs. It tells the team how its performance is to be judged (expectations and experiences) and by whom (customers). It tells the team if its work processes (relationships and operations) are effective. Without data from the outside, the team simply cannot perform, and low performance almost certainly will produce low morale.

MCEBO's Low Morale

One effect of MCEBO's general lack of alignment was that morale was distressingly low. Employees were having serious doubts about whether they wanted to work there. An underlying cause of this low morale was the company's lack of alignment around a shared vision and value system. As a result, it was difficult for individuals to feel aligned with the organization's purpose and values.

Another contributor to low morale was the lack of a clearly understood career development process. Employees wanted the company to establish a clear career development and evaluation process. In addition, rewards and recognitions did not reflect performance in the top three tiers, and employees wanted an incentive/profit sharing plan that included everyone. The MCEBO motto, "People are our most valuable asset," was not supported by action, and employees needed some serious demonstration of a genuine, long-term commitment from management. Consistently treating people with honesty, respect, and fairness enables the autonomy and collaboration necessary for high individual and collective performance.

Some key employees felt their work environment lacked openness, truth, and honesty. For example, MCEBO had few open forums for feedback. Dissenters were often not seen as team players. Many believed that being outspoken was a career detriment. Finally, the culture discouraged risk taking, experimentation, and open communication.

Another contribution to low morale was the perception that communications were ineffective, inconsistent, and filled with mixed messages. Management was unable or unwilling to disclose problems and situations fully. Managers were generally unavailable and had little personal interaction with employees.

Many also felt that MCEBO's leaders lacked focus and cooperation. The company had failed to develop, commit to, and stick to a good strategy. For instance, leaders vacillated between centralizing and decentralizing the management of various functions. The lack of consistent strategy created role confusion and made it difficult to measure individual performance. There was too much internal competition and not enough cooperation.

The nine windows of the Open Organization Model provided a framework for understanding MCEBO's morale problems and for intervening to create a climate with which people could identify. According to the model, high morale is possible only when employees feel committed to a goal that they value (unity) and when they are empowered (internal responsiveness) to attain that goal.

Openness and Quality as Organizational Strategies

Our research compels us to conclude that open, adaptive organizations have a competitive edge in a difficult, demanding economy. Open, adaptive organizations clearly outperform less flexible or culturally inappropriate organizations. The work of John

Kotter and James Heskett (1992) on organizational effectiveness supports this conclusion. These researchers were interested in discovering the nature of the relationship between the cultural appropriateness of an organization and its economic performance. At the end of their study, what emerged as the most consistent finding was that organizations that can adapt their culture to the context (or marketplace) in which they function are more profitable over the long run than companies that fail at this endeavor. If openness and quality are to become strategies of the organization, then top management must develop those strategies and provide the leadership for executing them.

We must remember, therefore, that a strategy is a plan or method to reach a goal and that valid strategies have several positive attributes. They:

- Provide methods to reach the goals of the organization
- Can be sustained over the long term
- Balance an internal with an external focus
- Integrate the various components or parts of the organization
- Remain useful despite changes in the marketplace
- Can be understood and practiced by all members of the organization

Openness and quality cannot simply be installed like new pieces of equipment. Rather they must be integrated into the organization over time and nurtured with competence, patience, friendly persuasion, and sincere caring.

Summary

In this chapter we have discussed the interdependence between quality relationships and unity of purpose and service. The organization must align around the shared purpose that emerges from an understanding of customer needs and requirements. Doing this requires continuous learning for MCEBO's employees as the business environment changes. Such continuous learning can occur only when individuals and groups are open and willing to change or to transform in order to provide quality products and services.

EIGHT

CHANGING FROM THE INDIVIDUAL OUT: THE CASE OF "CYCLOPS"

The case study in this chapter and the next describes an intervention from the individual level at a company we will refer to as Cyclops.

Some Historical Perspective

Cyclops was one of the world's largest oil exploration and production companies. It had developed state-of-the-art technologies for finding and producing oil and gas and had become a world leader in its marketplace. The organization produced software and provided related services to a variety of customers — many of which were operating companies within the parent company, and thus in-house. Its employees were both competent and knowledgeable about the business.

It was a time when few companies had the staff or technical resources to develop such technologies. The company president, who we will refer to as Rod Jones, had assembled a highly skilled group of geophysicists and computer scientists, and together this group created and deployed products that beat all competitors hands down. However, these technologies were so sophisticated that they required huge supercomputers to function.

That did not pose much of a problem initially. Customers had to rely on the company to help them collect and analyze the complex data required to find and produce oil and gas. They put up with delays and problems because there was no place else to go, and besides, the staff of the company really worked hard to help customers meet their needs.

Then the times changed. New, faster personal computers and PC networks became available, as did software packages for analyzing seismic and production data. Customers began to clamor for more cost-effective, timely systems to aid them in exploration and production activities. They communicated these needs to the company. But, sadly, Cyclops did not respond to their needs. Instead, the company responded to what it *wanted* its customers to need. As a consequence, customers began to experiment with other vendors who could provide them with the hardware and software they wanted, and the use of Cyclops products and services began to decline. Over several years, the company lost more and more customers.

Discovering the Problem

Our initial mission with Cyclops was to help it strategically align with the changing marketplace. We assembled the company's top eighteen executives and completed a strategic team development activity, the results of which were new vision and mission statements for Cyclops and a new set of values that stressed the importance of the customer and the need to empower all employees to better serve customers.

Customer Dissatisfaction

Cyclops then made an effort to find out why customers were dissatisfied. As a part of the strategic team development, a large study of customer satisfaction was undertaken. The primary question we wanted to address was *why* Cyclops had been losing customers. Table 8.1 summarizes the variables we measured.

What amazed us during the survey design phase was how difficult it was for Cyclops to identify its customers. The com-

Table 8.1. Determinants of Customer Satisfaction at Cyclops.

Variable Measured	Items Included
Company image—customer attitudes toward the organization	Customer perceptions of the organization's: • Customer-based quality mission • Emphasis on continuous improvement • Cooperation among units • Commitment to quality by senior management
Department image—customer attitudes toward a particular Cyclops unit	Customer perceptions of the unit's focus on: • Customer needs • Partnering relationships • Continuous improvement
Cost-effectiveness of products and services—customer perceptions that products and services are well worth the cost and that charges are *not* excessive	Customer perceptions of: • Value of products and services • Costs relative to competitors' products and services
Features of products and services—customer perceptions regarding how products and services meet, exceed, or fail in relation to customer expectations	Customer perceptions of: • Ease of use • Diversity of expertise • Consistency • Completeness • Pretesting to ensure accuracy
Technical support—customer perceptions about how well the staff provides technical support to customers	Customer perceptions of: • Support after delivery • Usefulness of documents • Reliability of information • Keeping customers informed with progress reports • Staff knowledge of products and services
Interpersonal style—customer perceptions of staff's interpersonal behavior and their perceived motives	Customer perceptions of: • Taking initiative to get things done • Willingness to help • Treating customers as important • Trustworthiness
Timeliness—customer perceptions of how quickly employees respond to customers and how easy it is to obtain products and support services	Customer perceptions of: • Ease of contacting staff • Delivery when promised • Speed of complaint resolution • Ease of access to computer hardware

pany simply did not know what people it should survey. The process of identifying the customer base took much precious time. Eventually, one thousand customers were asked to complete the survey. In addition, a sample of employees completed a similar survey so that customer perceptions could be compared to employee perceptions. The outcome variables in the survey were customer satisfaction and customer loyalty. Customer loyalty was measured in two ways: the intention to remain a committed customer and the actual use of competitors' products and services.

The results of this study were very clear: satisfied customers were more likely to remain customers and were less likely to have tried competitors' products and services. Dissatisfied customers, on the other hand, were less likely to remain customers and were much more likely to have used competitors' products and services. Customer dissatisfaction and the likelihood of going to a competitor were strongly and negatively correlated.

Customer Loyalty

Why do customers abandon a company? Our study revealed that nearly half of the variance in satisfaction ratings was accounted for by the following five variables:

1. *Organizational image.* Customers formed global perceptions of the company based on the extent to which they perceived its employees cared for their needs. (When company leaders are perceived to be uncaring and uncommitted to customers, customers tend to seek out and use alternative sources of products and services.)
2. *Product and service features.* The next most important variable was the specific features of the products and services used. Clearly, customers wanted features that met their needs.
3. *Technical support.* The third most important predictor was the technical features of the products and services the customers used.
4. *Interpersonal style.* The fourth most important factor was the style with which the company interacted with the customer.

5. *Interaction between product and service features and interpersonal style.* Finally, the interaction between the interpersonal style of the employees and the product and service features produced a relationship climate that either enhanced or inhibited customer loyalty.

Using these five factors, approximately four out of every five customers (85 percent) were classified as either satisfied or dissatisfied (using a two-group median split). Organizational image was by far the most powerful predictor, and, coincidentally, it is the factor most affected by leadership behaviors.

Thus, over time, Cyclops customers regarded the organization as unresponsive to their needs and concerns. Although they believed the organization to be extremely competent technically, they felt the company no longer cared for them as individuals with specific and significant problems. Despite the fact that individual relationships within the company were rated positively, the leader—and thus the organization—was perceived to be unresponsive to customer needs. Customers in turn sought out other suppliers and companies that would work with them to meet their individual needs in a timely manner.

The customers' concerns were certainly not unfounded. The environment at Cyclops was not responsive enough to their concerns. In fact, when we were presenting some feedback data from a customer survey, one member of the leadership team said, "That can't be true!" He did not believe the data could possibly be representative of Cyclops customers, so he simply dismissed it. Three months later, Cyclops was dissolved.

Determining and Applying
a Strategy to Address the Problem

The leaders of Cyclops said they wanted to improve the quality of products and services; however, this notion came more from an emphasis on quality at the conglomerate headquarters than from within Cyclops itself. So a decision was made to launch a quality improvement effort. Jones agreed to sponsor the effort, budgeted generously for it, hired an energetic leader, and provided two full-time staff. The strategy was twofold: (1) to train the organization in quality improvement tools and (2) to teach individual members of the executive leadership team about quality improvement and to implement any necessary changes.

In short, the leadership of Cyclops made an effort to change and to become more responsive to customers. With the help of outside consultants, they began a new participatory strategic planning process that was systematic and anchored to a broad base of customer information. This process itself was a great risk because the leadership had never been involved in a participatory approach to strategic planning.

The leadership also tried to reflect on their strengths and their needs for personal improvement. Clearly, the individual and collective will existed to improve the organization and to provide better, more relevant service to customers. But it never quite materialized and Cyclops died, not because it lacked the talent, but because the company president did not focus on the need for transformation or commit to it quickly enough.

The Real Heart of the Problem

Despite the ambitions of its junior management team to be a more democratic organization, Cyclops was ruled by a very powerful leader at the top. Rod Jones was not powerful by virtue of his outgoingness or persuasiveness but by virtue of his tendency to make all strategic decisions without consulting others. In other words, he displayed very little external responsiveness. He operated in this manner habitually. But he was producing unintended results. What had worked well for him in the past could not produce the desired results in the current situation.

When we analyze why Cyclops succumbed, what stands out is the lack of alignment between Jones's core values, his leadership team, and customer needs. What led to this lack of alignment? On the surface, at least, the problem was Jones's inability to lead the process of change. While he believed in the need for change, he could neither fully appreciate the depth of customer discontent nor hear the urgency of the need for change from his management team. Thus, the unconscious forces that guide people were clearly at play in the executive group. Jones was not the only problematic individual, however. There were two independent mavericks on the executive team who were wounded deep within their personality structure and who were easily triggered into anger, which became fairly dysfunctional for the group. When the group became unfocused, the two executives typically split into nonproductive pairs or subgroups, fought with one another, or withdrew. Thus the two drastically underutilized their abilities; they were too closed off and unable to solve problems when they felt threatened; and they had difficulty being helpful.

When it came to good, comprehensive decision making, they did reasonably well, as long as their decisions fell within the context of fairly routine problems. Whenever they had to deal with strange or unusual data, they had great difficulty, and Jones himself provided no help. Even under normal conditions, his tendency was to pay only cursory attention to team meetings and to spend much of his time away from the team. And this held true on the most critical issues.

Three Levels of Competence

Why did Jones have so much difficulty collaborating with others? This question can be answered in terms of competencies. Competence includes three components: (1) *knowledge,* (2) *attitudes and values* that support that knowledge so a person can act in his or her environment, and (3) *skills* to do the job. To provide competent customer service, one needs to have knowledge about customers, have an attitude and a value system that supports listening to customers and responding to their needs, and have skills for providing good customer service.

Some experts view competence from three levels: (1) *adaptive competencies,* which relate to how one approaches the challenge of living; (2) *functional competencies,* which relate to one's willingness and ability to solve problems, make decisions, plan, evaluate, relate, and so on; and (3) *job-specific skills,* which relate to the specific skills and values needed for the job in question.

There was no question about Jones's job-specific skills: he was a recognized expert on oil exploration and production. Likewise, there was no doubt about his functional skills. He was adept at solving problems and making decisions. However, at the adaptive level, when Jones was faced with nonroutine problems, he was often dysfunctional, as were many members of his executive team. For example, instead of being open to the survey data that contradicted his particular view of the world, Jones would deny its importance or discredit its validity; instead of listening to opinions that varied from his, he would withdraw or blame someone or something else for the problems he was experiencing. At the same time, he was a very able, caring, and committed person. However, neither Jones nor his staff seemed to be able to engage in meaningful discourse, strategic-creative problem solving, or learning that would enable them to lead the organization through transformation. They needed to examine the values and assumptions they were making that were generating the action strategies producing the poor results.

Jones (as well as his staff) did not know how to deal with pressure and stress and tended to become paralyzed with uncertainty when some change occurred, such as when customers began complaining about the company's lack of responsiveness to their immediate needs. Instead of being open to valid information—both facts and feelings—Jones would routinely seek the counsel of the company's customer advisory groups (comprised of top executives from customer companies), who themselves had problems tracking current developments in the field. Thus, he would take the counsel of those who were also out of touch with the real concerns of customers.

At the adaptive level—the level of one's basic beliefs about trust, competence, acceptance, and success—Jones clearly struggled. He wanted to convey these qualities to others because he clearly believed in them. However, his behavior was not congruent with his beliefs. In the parlance of action science, his *espoused theory* (what he said) and his *theory-in-use* (what he did) were incongruent. He and his team could not achieve the needed transformation because they were unable to transform themselves, their teams, and the organization to meet customer requirements.

Summary

In general, individuals who do not function well in relation to others have a negative influence on a team's ability to respond to one another as individuals. In almost any team where at least two individuals have difficulty functioning on an individual basis, there will be trouble developing the team into an effective unit. Nevertheless, we invested great time and energy and made tremendous progress in forming a clear vision for the group, a mission, key values, a much narrower focus on goals, and some key ground rules for working together. All of this work served to build a much stronger alignment of the executive group and initiated functions that started to improve customer service. They were, as a team, beginning to achieve a new level of team learning and problem solving. They simply ran out of time.

Although it was a very effective effort, in the end, it was too little too late. The president and the executive group failed to make the turnaround that was necessary for this service company to be deemed valuable by its parent organization. The customer base continued to shrink, profits fell below an acceptable level, and Cyclops was merged with two other service companies to form a new organization.

Chapter Nine will take a deeper look at individual unity, self-concept, and various personality factors that influence groups and organizations and will explain the interconnections between individual unity and the other components of the Open Organization Model. It contains ideas about what to consider in yourself as a leader of change and transformation, working toward a more open, adaptable organization.

NINE

ALIGNING PERSONAL AND ORGANIZATIONAL VALUES

The case of Cyclops and Rod Jones demonstrates how individual unity (window one) can affect the functioning of a whole group or organization (see Figure 9.1). More specifically, it demonstrates how the unique personality of a leader or group of leaders can have dire consequences for the way an entire organization functions. To fully appreciate the concept of individual unity, it is necessary to understand some basics about self-concept and human personality, which we overview in this chapter.

Factors Involved in Self-Concept

The term *self-concept* refers to the unique beliefs one has about oneself. Three sets of beliefs shape the self-concept:

1. Beliefs about reality—What is life like? What is real?
2. Beliefs about possibility—What does one expect from life? What can one do or not do?
3. Beliefs about value—What is good? Bad? What is worth striving for?

Figure 9.1. Values in the Open Organization Model.

	Unity	Internal responsiveness	External responsiveness
Individual	1 Values	2 Congruence	3 Connection
Group	4 Shared purpose	5 Quality relationships	6 Collaboration
Organization	7 Shared vision	8 Alignment	9 Contribution

An individual's unique self-concept is a product of his or her experiences. These experiences are a function of the nature and quality of the individual's environment interacting with his or her genetic capacities and personality. The person and the environment interact to produce behavior in the social world. The behavior produces consequences, which reinforce established patterns of social interaction. The person builds a cognitive structure, or pattern, for each operation required in his or her environment. As the person learns how to interact with the environment, each new cognitive pattern becomes associated or integrated with the existing patterns. The person's emerging view is what we call the *self-concept.*

Once a person's self-concept and unique frame of reference are formed, they shape and organize his or her experience. They serve to help form perceptual patterns such that the person sees and gets what they expect to see and get — or, from Mezirow's viewpoint (1991, p. 6), relates the experience to some preexisting frame of reference.

Determinants of the Self

Both the environment and the individual's unique personality and cognitive structures shape the emerging self-concept. The individual brings his or her unique personality to every situation, and, out of this interaction, emerges with that self-concept more or less the same. Significant alterations in adult thinking and behavior patterns seem to occur with critical examination of the values, goals, assumptions, and premises that influence one's interactions.

An individual's personality is comprised of three kinds of traits, each interacting with one another and with the environment:

1. Temperament traits describe the individual's basic moods and orientations toward the environment. For example, some individuals are shy while others are outgoing; some individuals are threat sensitive while others are threat resistant.
2. Motivational or dynamic traits refer to the individual's motivations and needs, such as the need for mastery and control or the need for dominance and power.
3. Ability traits refer to the individual's ability to learn and specific aptitudes for verbal, numerical, abstract, mechanical, and spatial reasoning.

We can conclude that the self-concept is one's unique set of beliefs about reality, possibility, and value in relation to one's environment. The self-concept shapes one's:

- Values and beliefs, which influence the premises one forms,
- Pattern or style of interacting with others,
- Strategies, and, ultimately,
- The results one achieves.

These relationships are illustrated in Figure 9.2.

Figure 9.2. Foundations of the Self-Concept.

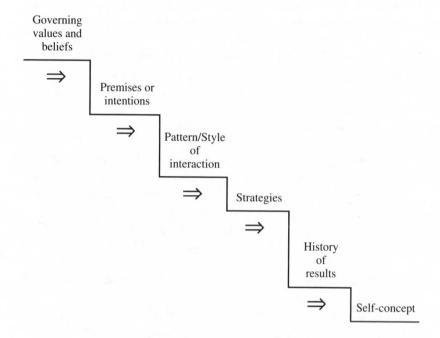

Operating in Context

The postulate that individuals operate in relation to their context is the basis for the Open Organization Model. To be healthy and fully functioning, people must know who they are (self-concept, unity), be aware of their context (external responsiveness), and be constantly able to organize and reorganize their life structure so that they live congruently with their own self-concept (internal responsiveness, critical reflection, or examination of premises and frames of reference). This awareness carries over to the context of groups and organizations: to operate effectively in a group or organization, an individual's uniqueness must be congruent with the context of the group or organization.

In other words, people must be able to express, in the context of the team and the organization, that which makes each of them unique. They must be able to live their values and realize their dreams within that context. The team and the organization must therefore provide the context in which such uniqueness can be expressed. Likewise, an individual must choose or create contexts that empower him or her to be their true self. And, alternatively, the team and the organization must choose individuals who are able and willing to live in their group's particular context. Shared values become the primary organizers, or the "glue," of group cohesiveness.

Individuals both create their contexts and are created by them. With this life structure in mind, we can begin to understand personality dynamics. When we examine individuals and their environments, we can start making connections between their personality dynamics and their unique transactions with those environments.

Individual Unity

Unity may therefore be viewed as the organized wholeness, centered on self-concept, that a person brings to a situation and that helps to shape his or her goals in that situation. Unity also influences how that person reaches those goals. Unity is the degree to which the person has aligned his or her unique cognitive structure, temperament, abilities, traits, attitudes, preferences, beliefs, and core values with the demands of life. It is the ability of the person to express his or her essence in the context in which he or she lives. Unity as conceptualized here has a self-organizing capacity. It constitutes the basis for any form of social interaction — conscious or unconscious — for once routine patterns have been firmly established, they no longer reside in conscious awareness.

Unity at the individual level means successful alignment of the individual and the individual's life experiences around a set of core values. Individual unity, centeredness, or personal congruence has been an issue in human life from the first moment of recorded history. When we talk about individual unity, we refer not only to the importance of being unified around core values but also to the importance of behaving so that life is congruent with those core values. This process involves both being centered, or unified, and being able to maintain that centeredness. Many, if not all, personal growth experiences reestablish some congruence between core values and everyday lives or lead individuals to reexamine their core values and the premises that influence their behavior and others' behavior.

Human Personality

Personality can be defined in terms of behavior. From this point of view, a person's personality allows you to predict what she or he will do in a given situation. Another way of describing personality is in terms of individual behavior patterns such as reasoning or ability to tolerate ambiguity. From this point of view, personality is the way in which someone has learned to adapt to the process of living. It is the sum total of the individual's experiences and everything that the individual has learned while trying to cope with the challenges of a full life.

So what is it that determines how and what an individual learns? According to most modern theories of personality, an individual's behavior in any given situation is a function of his or her unique ability, dynamic, and temperament traits, his or her expectations that a given behavior will lead to a given outcome, his or her values and attitudes about what is important and worth striving for, and the opportunities and threats inherent in a given situation—the force field of influencing phenomena.

In other words, you, as an individual, must be able to express in the team and the organization context that which makes you unique. You must be able to live your values and realize your dreams within that context. The team and the organization must therefore ultimately provide the context in which such uniqueness can be expressed. Likewise, it is necessary for you to choose or create contexts that empower you to be who you truly are. And, alternatively, it is necessary for the team and the organization to choose individuals who are able and willing to live in the particular context of the team and organization. Typically, neither process is done well. As we saw in Chapter Eight, Rod Jones was an excellent fit for his organization for the better part of thirty years. When the technical and user environments changed radically, Jones failed to adapt; he did not transform himself as these changes required. Rather than aligning the organization with its customers' needs, Jones and his team members continued with their outdated practices. The customers simply went elsewhere.

Individuals both create their contexts and are created by their contexts. It is in the context of this life structure that one can begin to explain personality dynamics. When you examine the person and his or her environment, you can begin to make connections between personality dynamics and the individual's unique transactions with his or her environment.

When we talk about unity, we must therefore talk about values. Values have been defined as beliefs that guide actions. What a person values is revealed in what that person does. People may not always behave in accordance with their values, even though they say they value something. For instance, Rod Jones said he valued collaboration; however, he made many unilateral decisions, often without consulting anyone. Values may be observed at three different levels:

1. Acceptance — At this level, the person accepts a value as important and communicates its importance to others. For example, Rod Jones often spoke about the need for collaboration in an organization committed to total quality management.
2. Preference — At this level, the person chooses one value over another when given the opportunity to do so, such as when ranking the importance of different values on a survey. For example, Jones said he believed that collaboration was more important than unilateral action.
3. Commitment — At this level, the person consciously chooses to live a value, makes a public commitment to do so, and can be observed living this value across a wide range of situations in a consistent pattern (Simon, Howe, and Kirschenbaum, 1972). At the commitment level, if Jones had truly valued collaboration, he could have been seen discussing issues with his people, asking them to help evaluate alternatives, and so on.

It is said that level 1 and level 2 reflect espoused values, while level 3 represents a true value on which one might act. A true value is one that guides behavior.

One characteristic of unity, then, is that a person's observable behavior is organized around and congruent with his or her consciously chosen set of core values. In the book *Passages* (1976), Gail Sheehy discusses unity as one of the core characteristics of the self-actualized person.

Milton Rokeach (1968) described two kinds of values: *process (instrumental) values* and *outcome (terminal) values.* Outcome values are the ends toward which we strive, while process values are the means by which we attain outcome values. Whatever we hold as an outcome value — for example, a world at peace — will cause us to behave in ways that contribute toward world peace. Our behavior reveals our process values.

Another aspect of individual unity is that, as you center your life-style and behavior around your core values, whenever you have a life experience that is inconsistent with your core values, you will be uncomfortable until you can resolve the lack of congruence between what you are experiencing and your values. When our behaviors are not aligned with our espoused values, we experience dissonance or live in a state of denial, and either one impedes our effectiveness. To remain centered and healthy, it is crucial that we, as individuals, create and maintain alignment between the values we have incorporated into our self-concept and the behaviors we exhibit.

There are two kinds of gaps between behaviors and values that can cause problems. The first is a gap between your core values and the values endorsed by your organization. For example, if you are working in an environment where a value you believe in (like truth, trust, or simplicity) is not explicit or is violated, then you develop a disturbance because of the lack of congruence between the context and what you value as an individual. Abraham Maslow (1971) called this disturbance a *metapathology.*

A gap between your espoused values and your behavior can also lead to *incongruence.* For example, Rod Jones espoused collaboration but then acted unilaterally. This incongruence may have occurred because he was not conscious of his core beliefs.

Why do people sometimes choose to act in ways that are inconsistent with their true values? Almost every therapist has observed that people often do things that are at variance with what they say they believe, even though it causes them pain. As it turns out, a person's true values often become:

- Lost in the unconscious mind
- Hidden as they try to conform to the reality they perceive
- Denied as they try to conform to their expectations of what they should be like

There are many possible process and outcome values; however, we can only fulfill a limited number of priorities. Thus, our values are arranged into a kind of mental hierarchy, and the top five to seven values in our priority list become the core values that influence our decisions and actions. It is therefore important to understand our priority values and to behave in ways congruent with those values.

Carl Rogers (1961, 1969, 1970, 1989) believed that every one of us is born with the potential to become fully functioning. He called this potential our "actualizing tendency." To realize this inherent potential, however, we must be exposed to an environment that is nurturing or enabling. Such environments are typically characterized by unconditional positive regard, genuineness and openness, empathic understanding, and warmth.

However, many of us receive conditional regard—regard that is contingent on conforming to a certain standard or pattern. Thus, over time, we tend to forget who we really are and live according to how we think we should be—wearing a facade. Once an idealized, fictitious self-concept forms, our behaviors tend to conform to our expectations for this substitute real self. We tend to achieve our needs or fulfill our own goals in ways that match false expectations. This is the origin of the dissonance or incongruence between the real self and idealized self, between espoused values and behavior. This gap is experienced as pain or dissonance. When the gap between real self and idealized self is recognized, we typically are energized for learning and transformation.

To be truly responsive to our external world, to reach out and have contact with others, to build close friendships, and to have healthy loving relationships, we must be centered and be living a congruent life. We must know what our values are and live consistently with those values. Only then can we reach out, truly relate to, and contribute to another person's life.

A good example of how this responsiveness operates is our case with Rod Jones. To better understand his lack of responsiveness and the effects it had on the organization, we will examine his personality in more detail.

The president could be characterized as being intelligent, reserved and aloof, controlling yet shy, and extremely self-sufficient. Most of the top eight people at Cyclops could be characterized similarly.

We mention these characterizations in light of recent studies of leadership success. For years, people have debated whether leaders are born or made and whether specific and measurable traits exist that can be associated with effective leadership. The data are still far from conclusive; however, it does seem clear that certain enduring personality traits do affect leadership behavior.

Personality Factors and Leadership Success

A study of 105 men and women who had failed as leaders was conducted to determine whether any specific personality traits could be associated with the "failed" executive. Researchers administered the Sixteen Personality Factor Questionnaire and the Helson Leadership Effectiveness Inventory to a group of executives, some of whom were very successful and some of whom had failed (defined in this study as being fired by their board of directors due to the poor performance of their organizations).

Analysis of these personality profiles revealed that several traits distinguished "failed" from "successful" executives. First of all, researchers found that failed executives tended to be reserved and aloof. They exhibited very little warmth toward others, had little need for them, and were more inclined to seek data from their own internal worlds and feelings as opposed to seeking input from outside sources. Jones was clearly viewed by his subordinates as being "aloof."

A second characteristic typical of these men and women was a tendency or need to be very controlling of their social environments, which made it difficult for them to empower others to make decisions. Instead, these executives tended to make unilateral decisions, even when they espoused the value of collaboration. Jones was consistently criticized by some subordinates for not "walking the talk."

The tendency toward aloofness and the need for control were accompanied by a tendency to be socially shy and threat sensitive. Not only did these individuals tend to avoid social contact, which they found somewhat painful, but also they avoided debate in any form, especially if the debate engendered conflict and such feelings as anger. On some occasions these men and women suppressed any show of conflict; on others they withdrew the moment the conflict emerged.

Finally, the failed executives in the study exhibited an extreme degree of self-reliance. They had very little need for the support of others and seldom sought support when making decisions and solving problems. At Cyclops, unilateral decision making was the norm, even though the executives espoused collaboration. When push came to shove, the president made all of the strategic decisions, usually on the basis of data that was valid some ten years earlier. Executives were clearly too reliant on "self" to formulate an effective leadership team.

Functions of Leadership

How do these traits influence behavior that leads to failure? Warren Bennis (1984) says that two of the most important functions of leaders are to build shared meaning and to develop a climate of trust. Given these functions, we can better understand how the leaders at Cyclops failed to realize their visions. For one, because they were so self-sufficient, they felt little need to communicate their vision in terms that others could understand and commit to. Jones clearly felt little need to share what he envisioned and had little inclination to work with others to ensure that the organization was aligned around this vision. More significantly, because he was so aloof and shy, he was unaware of the great divisions among his senior management team about the vision, and he was unaware of how greatly the external world had changed. Customers no longer wanted overengineered products, no matter how elegant they were. They wanted timely, simple solutions to the problems they dealt with on a daily basis. And, because of Jones's tendency toward self-reliance, he did not interact with others in a way that engendered trust and confidence in his ability to lead.

The significance of this leadership behavior was revealed in a study of the company's customers. External customers came to believe that Jones did not care for them and eventually doubted his ability to create an organization that could meet their needs. As the leader of Cyclops, Jones set the tone for an unwillingness to listen to customers.

During his lifetime, he had developed the competencies that were required of a successful leader in the organization required at a specific time. However, the marketplace and the greater socioeconomic climate changed dramatically. Even though the pressures to change increased exponentially, Jones did not experience himself as a person who needed to learn or change. Instead, he reinforced the status quo by refusing to listen to his staff and by denying the overwhelming evidence that suggested the company was in grave danger. Only those persons who were in direct contact with customers seemed aware of the dissonance between customer needs and expectations and the products and services Cyclops provided. Cyclops was following its same old routine, independent of environmental challenges, technological changes, and customer requirements.

The Cyclops story clearly illustrates the interdependent nature of organizational life. Jones's leadership behavior — a function of his own values and beliefs — profoundly influenced how the executive management team functioned. It reduced internal responsiveness to almost zero. Jones's self-reliance reinforced excessive self-reliance among many of the members of the management team. His unwillingness or discomfort in dealing with conflict reinforced this tendency toward unilateral action, resulting in very little cooperation among the members of the management team. It took them forever to make even simple decisions; once made, key decisions were often not implemented.

Of more significance, this splintering of the management team had a profound effect on the external responsiveness of the Cyclops organization. It made it almost impossible for the organization to appreciate fully the significance and extent of the change in customer needs. Thus, employees tried to work harder and harder to meet customer needs when what they should have been doing was learning a new paradigm, one that was based on the customer, responsiveness, and cost-effectiveness. That would have involved doing things differently instead of doing more of the same. Because the organization was very low in external responsiveness, it did not make use of the customer data, the company was disbanded, and many people suffered as a result.

Summary

Cyclops needed to reframe its mission but the lack of unity on the management team, especially a lack of unity between the organization's values and the leader's true values, created a situation in which the leaders were unable and unwilling to do so in time to save the company. Skills and knowledge lacking the values that align with the surrounding environment or context often fail to provide what an enterprise needs to survive and prosper in a changing, competitive environment.

Cyclops was an organization with great potential: its employees' knowledge and skills were superb, but the president's value system mitigated against monitoring customer needs and having true dialogue or discourse with the customer base in order to meet or exceed their expectations. Thus, over a three-year period, Cyclops went out of business. Jones retired, another key executive was "separated," others were "outplaced," and hundreds of others lost their jobs.

TEN

CONCLUSION: OPEN ORGANIZATIONS AND CONTINUOUS RENEWAL

The situations at PGM, MCEBO, and Cyclops are not atypical of U.S. multinational companies, which have done a very good job when dealing with a reasonably stable environment. But in this post-Newtonian or post-Descartian world of ours, we must be aware of the chaos evolving in the marketplace and within our society, and we need to be highly flexible and interact with information and energy surges from our environment. We must also be able to lead our organizations from one transformation to the next — or from one state of disequilibrium toward stability — as often as necessary to remain relevant to the marketplace. Then we must be able to return to disequilibrium and remodify our organizations so that our strategies and our customers' changing needs are always aligned. Otherwise, we will probably not sustain any degree of competitive advantage.

Elements of Open, Continuous Improvement Cultures

Openness and quality will not take root unless some important elements are in place. Achieving the kind of performance exemplified by the very best organizations is possible only when

131

an organization enables individual autonomy, learning, risk taking, and problem solving. To do so, an organization must have:

- A constancy of purpose as revealed in a clear strategic direction
- A philosophy of cooperation and teamwork
- A desire for continuous improvement and learning and a system for implementing continuous improvement
- Alignment and management of key performance subsystems
- Effective leadership of change

Constancy or Unity of Purpose

It is vital that an organization have a clear strategic direction that is communicated and accepted by everyone in the organization. Clear strategic direction must precede other initiatives. In fact, constancy of purpose is the first of W. Edwards Deming's fourteen points (1986). Focus and clear strategic direction is about organizational effectiveness — *doing the right things*. It requires being both market- and values-driven. It is defined in terms of marketplace needs and which of those needs the organization intends to fulfill, now and in the future. To enable success and sustained competitive advantage, the organization, its leaders, and the marketplace needs must be aligned.

A Philosophy of Cooperation

When an organization is viewed as a system of linkages between and among processes, each of which is designed to fulfill the needs that underlie its mission, it is easy to see that the only way an organization can succeed is through cooperation and teamwork.

All employees — at every level — should understand their contribution to the aims of the organization. All must do their part to improve processes and systems to better serve customers — both external and internal. The foundation of such a commitment is individual learning and transformation. All individuals facing nonroutine events must master the art of critical reflection, examining their own assumptions, premises, and frames of reference.

Continuous Improvement and Learning

The need for continuous improvement and learning creates two critical interrelated goals: achieving continuous improvement and learning, and designing and implementing the learning systems that will support them.

The Desire for Continuous Improvement

With respect to the first issue, the successful organization aligns around the desire for continuous improvement. In other words, continuous improvement must be an intrinsic core value of that organization. It does not just happen. For openness and quality to be an effective organizational strategy and for people to engage in the continuous improvement process, they must be intrinsically motivated to improve the system and its products and services. This intrinsic motivation comes from:

- A belief in and commitment to an organization's purpose and aims
- Management and leadership behaviors and processes that empower people to engage in continuous improvement
- Support for accomplishment, including time, tools, and other resources
- Systems that enable people to take pride in their accomplishment
- People capable of and skilled in critical reflection

Continuous Learning Systems

We have some clues as to the types of systems that are best positioned for learning and the kinds of processes that will support members to be continuous learners. The system needs to have:

1. The right culture—that is, a system with a set of beliefs that are publicly articulated in its mission statement. The statement must include values that support both organizational goals and individual goals. There should be a norm that promotes learning within the system, along with risk

taking and creative problem solving. Learning must be highly valued. Critical reflection skills must be learned and applied.

2. A mechanism for confronting norms and organizational values, through its planning, resource allocation, and decision-making processes.
3. A centralized, organic structure that provides for flexible decision making and that allows for shifts in beliefs and actions.
4. An identifiable strategic posture in its environment that sets boundaries for interpreting the organization's environment and that creates some momentum for change.
5. Characteristics of a participative learning system — that is, a system with institutionalized participation in decision making, which heightens the probability that decision makers are exposed to one another's assumptions and beliefs on various issues (Morgan and Ramirez, 1983).

This kind of learning system organizes itself by sharing purpose and meaning with its members and its environment. It is holistic and driven by hope, rather than based on fear. Such a system welcomes change and shares the responsibility for managing it. The organization as a whole and its individual members have a high tolerance for ambiguity. Because of that, the system experiments frequently and views "errors" as important information sources rather than as mistakes. It values the intuitive skills of its employees and fosters their creativity.

In such an organization, members develop special skills. They see the rich interrelationships between the parts of the organization and manage boundaries rather than simply maintain them. Decisions are collaborative, not made from the top down. Rather than having all the answers and determining what everyone will do, managers shift toward asking stimulating questions and letting others discover what to do. Individuals are skilled at recognizing patterns and integrated wholes, rather than assuming linear, cause-effect relationships. Paradoxical thinking is encouraged, and "conflict" is reframed as "creative tension." Members, in learning how to learn, experience their own personal transformation.

Moving Toward Open Organizations

An open system with full interaction among all its parts and with its environment has resources for renewal. In a changing environment, this system must also be purposive, working toward specific short- or long-term goals.

The goal of development is organizational and societal renewal. Renewal will occur by developing organizations that deal effectively with uncertainty, diversity, and complexity. The development of open organizations requires a change process that is significantly different from traditional approaches.

1. *From authority to leadership.* An open organization does not rely on raw authority, policy making, or incentives in the usual sense. Full use of informal influence, communication, and goal setting is assumed. Various constituencies are involved in decision making.

2. *From tangible development to sociocultural development.* Development in traditional institutions tends to deal with tangible factors, such as finances and facilities, and to place less energy into changes in sociocultural and sociopolitical forms. The open organization focuses on change in the entire sociotechnical (human, technical, and strategic) system. Any satisfactory development plan involves total institutional renewal in all major components of the system and their relationships.

3. *From partial change strategies to comprehensive change strategies.* Typical change strategies focus on a single method or innovation, shifting personnel or units on the organizational chart, responding to immediate pressures or crises, or starting new units or programs. An open organization approach toward development in an established institution would be as broad as in a new institution.

4. *From identification with specialized knowledge to knowledge application systems.* Instead of focusing on a single idea that may soon be obsolete, open institutions install systems and roles (for instance, research and development) for selecting, introducing, and adapting a wide variety of ideas and practices. The challenge is to encourage learning processes that

can quickly lead to the application of new knowledge and technology.

5. *From simple change models to more complex systemic analysis and action taking.* Changes are complex social processes. Planned change usually involves risk, conflict, and ambiguity during initial stages. The pain and danger accompanying such change is matched, however, by the cost of changes forced upon an unprepared institution. Paradoxically, organizations undergoing change will have more conflict, mobilization, and confusion, yet be better "managed" than organizations that do not deal with change.

6. *From stability-weighted organizations to change-weighted organizations.* For some, concepts such as "planned change" or "change agents" are undesirable because they appear to value change itself. However, without planned change, an organization tends to drift toward an irrational and dangerous status quo reinforced by bureaucracy. Planned change assumes organizational lag and sets up mechanisms to counteract it. An ongoing capacity for constructive change is crucial for organizations of the future.

Applying the Open Organization Model

The Open Organization Model describes, in both general and specific terms, the ingredients for a successful organization. Quite simply, a high-performing, open organization is

- Unified from top to bottom around a shared and commonly understood vision (purpose), mission, values, and assumptions,
- Responsive to the needs and requirements of the context in which it functions (customers, the community, the society),
- Responsive to its own needs and capacities,
- Able to learn from its experiences and to change over time.

The Open Organization Model aids in developing an open, adaptive organization by providing a framework for understanding how organizations learn and grow. It can help you determine where your organization currently is, what its strengths and weaknesses are, and what must be done to create and sustain a high-performance culture.

In conclusion, movement from a closed to an open organization involves a shift from management control and coordination toward worker control and personal responsibility, fulfilled through interconnected worker teams. This shift creates a dilemma: on the one hand, such worker groups need much freedom and autonomy; on the other hand, it requires a high degree of openness between interconnected components. Without such openness, the organization cannot be responsive to customers and their needs or to larger sociocultural issues such as equality and diversity.

The Open Organization Model offers a framework that supports both routine and nonroutine activities. This optimizes adaptability and enhances learning on all levels: individual, group, and organization. Our model supports free and informed choice, personal empowerment, and self-management by each individual. The model also provides principles, norms, and structural processes that optimize the use of self-directed work teams. Individuals who are centered on values that are congruent with those of the organization and who connect well with other team members provide the foundation of an effective team. Teams with a clear, shared purpose and good interpersonal relationships can reach out and collaborate with others more effectively. When healthy people who share a vision can work openly with others, they can align themselves and perform at outstanding levels. They can then transform the organization to stimulate meaningful contributions both internally and externally.

Our work and the case studies presented in this book demonstrate processes that produce valuable results. The Open Organization Model provides a powerful framework to help you diagnose and, when necessary, ultimately transform your organization. We hope you will find it useful in your work.

RESOURCES FOR
OPEN ORGANIZATIONS

A

AN OVERVIEW OF
SYSTEMS THINKING

The philosophical perspective and operating principles of an
open organization come from the process philosophy of Alfred
North Whitehead (1933), from several aspects of group theory
in mathematics, and from general systems thinking. Process
philosophy views human life as organic and fluid rather than
mechanistic, as dependent on personal and group relationships
rather than simple cause-and-effect relationships, and as both
intuitive and rational. Systemic thinking de-emphasizes structure as the basis for organization. Instead, it focuses on goals,
functions, and processes, including self-organization and interaction in a diverse global economy.

This appendix overviews the concept of systems thinking and distinguishes between two grand thinking paradigms:
mechanistic and organismic. An understanding of systems thinking and these two paradigms will enhance your ability to view
organizations as open systems.

What Do We Mean by "Systems"?

To clarify our terminology, *systems* are abstract models that explain some aspect of the world and how things operate. They

define sets of *elements* that have a particular identity. These elements consist of any objects, boundaries, or relations that can be articulated. Systems are distinguished from the rest of the world by *boundaries*. Boundaries separate individual elements of the system as well. They may be attached to core ideas, such as different shapes, attributes, or times. Boundaries define the *relations* among sets of elements. Relations associate similar elements, such as like shapes or shared boundaries. In human groups, for instance, relations may involve affection or power. A system frames the rules that govern relations over time or form. These rules concern the *causes* or explanations of how and why something is a certain way at a certain time and place. For instance, a cause might be a precedent, a presence, or an absence. Finally, a system as a whole has qualities that differ from those of its parts. For example, when combined in the right proportion, the elements hydrogen and oxygen become water. These combined elements have a quality of wetness that the individual molecules do not have alone (Hutchinson and McWhinney, 1992, p. 3). In the same manner, an organization's culture is composed of various elements — its shared beliefs and stated values as well as the patterns of behavior seen in its norms and rewards. Together these elements create one's experience of culture as a dynamic, interactive whole that consists of something other than its individual elements.

A systems perspective is useful for studying organizations because it provides an overall framework or unifying quality that integrates the various facets of an organization. This approach allows us to examine the forces — both internal and external — that have a bearing on or explain its performance. Consequently, it becomes easier to build models and graphic representations of the relationships among the elements of the system and the system's environment.

Systems Thinking

The terms *systems thinking, systems approach,* and *systems perspective* are used frequently and interchangeably in contemporary organizational development literature. They usually indicate that some aspects of general systems theory were drawn upon to examine an organization. However, systems thinking has a broader and deeper conceptual history. Systems thinking is actually a "metadiscipline": it can be applied as a tool within other disciplines. One of its central concepts is that a "system" is a set of elements connected together to form a whole. The properties of the system are properties of the whole and not simply properties of its individual parts. So, to say that one is using a "systems approach" to a problem is a popularized way of saying that a particular problem is being examined by using some of the principles underlying the existence of whole entities.

Systems thinking has been emerging since 1945 and has been growing in its influence, so much so that Peter Checkland (1981) refers to a "systems movement" to describe the application of its concepts to a wide range of disciplines. It has been particularly powerful in examining change and complexity in human organizations. To understand this relatively new way of viewing the world, it is important to recognize that a systems approach, itself, is already deeply grounded in a set of beliefs about "how things work." That is to say, it reflects a new paradigm.

Shifting Paradigms

The way we see the world, and therefore define reality, has been deeply influenced by centuries of patterns of thinking. The particular worldview, or paradigm, out of which we operate is usually so embedded in our lives that we do not even realize it exists. Moreover, we may even be influenced by more than one paradigm. Paradigms help us explain how the world works. They provide order, meaning, a sense of control, and ownership in the culture. They evolve to help us explain aspects of our reality, for example, cause, time, space, control, change, and other relationships. Various authors have described the major paradigms that have been operating over the last one thousand years (Pepper, 1942; Kuhn, 1970; Capra, 1982; McWhinney, 1992). One of these authors, Thomas Kuhn, has observed that we are currently in a transition between two major worldviews. That is, we are in the process of a paradigm shift in which we are actively creating new myths, practices, and theories about our reality. The nature of this new worldview incorporates greater levels of interconnectedness and interdependence than assumed by previous scientific and social models of the universe.

Fritjof Capra (1982) has described the shift from the older mechanistic paradigm to the newer organismic paradigm. The *mechanistic* paradigm, which is strongly shaped by Newtonian physics and the thinking of French philosopher and scientist René Descartes, views the scientific method as the only valid approach to knowledge. It sees the universe as a mechanical system (like a giant clock) composed of elementary material building blocks and views life in society as a competitive struggle for existence. It emphasizes control over others through structure and hierarchy and reflects a belief that unlimited material progress can be achieved through economic and technological growth.

The *organismic* paradigm, on the other hand, reflects the philosophical influences of Plato and Aristotle. It sees the human spirit as the mode of consciousness through which we will become aware of the entire human species. It takes a systems approach that integrates the whole inseparably with the parts. Its holistic, "deep ecology" perspective views humans as interconnected to all other life systems and requires them to assume a more balanced role in the planetary ecosystem. It emphasizes *influence among* the parts of the system as the most effective mode of organizing rather than *dominance over* those parts. Consequently, the hierarchical structure of many systems will be replaced by a more adaptive structure—the network.

Table A.1 reflects the different modes of thinking and values in these two paradigms. One glance reveals their interrelationships.

General Systems Theory

The application of general systems theory to the field of organizational development and management provides a framework for integrating an otherwise overwhelming amount of information

Table A.1. Mechanistic Versus Organismic Thinking.

	Mechanistic	*Organismic*
Thinking	rational	intuitive
	analysis	synthesis
	reduces into parts	deals with wholes
	linear	non-linear
Values	self-assertive	integrative
	competitive	collaborative
	control	network
	expansion	conservation
	quantity	quality
	dominance	partnership

Source: Adapted from Capra, lecture notes, 1988, and Capra and Steindl-Rast, 1991.

about any one organization. It also offers a tool for identifying the major forces and variables that influence the functioning of an organization, from both an internal and an external perspective.

The concept of organizations as systems is rooted in general systems theory. General systems theory emerged in the late 1950s and early 1960s in reaction to the tendency to compartmentalize the various scientific disciplines. Its earliest thinking is credited to Ludwig von Bertalanffy, who originally published his concept of general systems theory in 1945.

Subsequently, a group of researchers began a search for a body of theory that would provide some unity to studies in various scientific areas as well as share the insights and theoretical concepts from the individual disciplines on a widespread basis. The central unifying concept they identified was the notion of a "system," loosely defined as a set of related objects with related attributes. It was felt that each of these disciplines must deal with systems of some sort and that some basic concepts were probably relevant to systems of all kinds. For instance, the concept of isomorphism suggests that a body of theoretical principles can be applied usefully to systems of all kinds and from all disciplines. Historically, general systems theory has involved the process of identifying those basic principles and applying them to specific systems of interest in various fields of study. The work in this field is highly synthetic — that is, it involves contributions from separate disciplines in the natural and social sciences.

Principles of Systems Thinking

Principles of systems thinking include concepts and polarities of concepts that describe, explain, and predict the behavior of a general system in four broad categories:

1. *Systemic* and *descriptive factors* make distinctions, classify, and outline the basic structure and processes of different types of systems. The concepts deal with types of systems, their internal organization, and their surroundings. Some of the factors are open and closed systems, interdependence, subsystems, and boundaries. All of these factors are incorporated in the Open Organization Model (or nine-window model), albeit the phenomena depicted are neither two-dimensional nor limited to nine windows. Depending on the nature and level of analysis, you can create as many windows as necessary to fit the dimensions of the entity you wish to analyze.

2. *Regulation* and *maintenance factors* deal with control and stabilization of the system. These include stability, feedback, and self-regulation. The Open Organization Model helps identify where breakdowns have occurred and where tension exists in these regulating processes.

3. *Dynamics* and *change* deal with the problems of nondisruptive change, responses to altered environmental conditions, and internally generated processes such as adaptation, learning, growth, and change. The Open Organization Model is designed to examine the internal and external conditions. The unity dimension addresses the system's ability to change and to maintain order simultaneously.

4. *Decline* and *breakdown* are two of the system's responses to its environment. They manifest themselves in stress, overload, and positive entropy. When an organization examines its unity, it can better align itself to respond to factors that might affect its decline. And when an organization assesses

its internal and external responsiveness, it can reduce the loss of energy that accompanies stress and decline.

The Systems Perspective

When we view an organization from a systems perspective, we assume that whatever "system" we are examining is composed of parts and that the parts are interrelated for some purpose or reason. The system is an organized, complex whole. The following concepts are assumed in that approach.

Holism. The organization should be considered as a functioning whole. This concept requires that we consider the performance of all components of the organization when we introduce change into any one component of the system. The Open Organization Model helps us examine the organization as a whole by analyzing the dimensions of unity and internal and external responsiveness. Given this property of holism, the model can focus initially at any level (for example, individual, group, organization, community) or any dimension (unity, internal or external responsiveness, or structural, symbolic, political, human resource) and still see the dynamics of the entire system.

Interdependence. The parts of the organization will be interdependent; therefore, if a change occurs in one part of the organization, it will influence all other parts of the organization, either directly or indirectly. The Open Organization Model looks at the various interrelationships among the subsystems at the individual, group, and organization levels.

Synergism. All parts of the system working together create an interactive effect that is greater than the sum of those parts working separately. An open organization displays synergism at peak performance.

Subsystems. The analysis of subsystems within a system is related to the concept of holism. Subsystems are groups of functioning elements within the larger system. What constitutes a "subsystem" depends upon the level of abstraction desired at a given point in time and the purpose of the analysis. The concept allows us to telescope back and forth in the perspective we take. The unit of analysis determines the subsystems. For instance, the Open Organization Model can focus on the individual, the work groups, the division, or the entire organization, community, conglomerate, or humankind, while examining the dimensions of unity and internal and external responsiveness.

Open-Closed. The degree of interaction an organization has with its environment can be described in terms of its openness. An open system is one that interacts with its environment, usually a larger system. Its boundaries are permeable, and information and resources flow freely across them. In contrast, a closed system has little or no interaction with its environment. Information is tightly controlled and resources are not shared. In truth, few systems are completely closed systems and few are completely open. It is, therefore, useful to think of this dimension on a continuum from closed to open or from maintaining continuity to cultivating change. All biological and social systems are open systems. They affect, and are affected by, their environment.

The degree to which a system is open varies at any given point in time. For example, an individual, healthy person can be considered an open system. Under stress, however, some individuals close up and cannot hear advice or criticism or respond to a threatening situation. They are not interacting with their environment; they are functioning more as a closed system. For instance, a co-worker may be living congruently with his or her values but be deeply wounded because of the loss of a loved one or the breakup of a significant relationship. In such a case, that individual's ability to express genuine warmth and caring for another person is impaired — sometimes for eighteen months or longer. The tendency for a system to be more closed, particularly when under stress or threat, helps explain why productivity drops in organizations that are downsizing. The "surviving" group of employees becomes depressed by the loss of fellow employees and friends. Because the model can be used to diagnose the degree to which an organization is open and interacting with its environment, it helps identify where in the system processes are stuck.

Static-Dynamic. This property describes the degree of change occurring within the system over time. A static system does not change; however, a dynamic system changes over time. Again, this concept is more useful when viewed on a continuum. Most biological and social systems are dynamic. For example, a university is a very dynamic system. Each year a new group of students enters the system and another group exits through graduation or attrition. Curriculum changes to keep pace with expanding knowledge, teaching methods improve, faculty and staff may change, and even physical facilities may shift to accommodate the student body.

State Maintenance. When an organization reacts in a specific way to an internal or external event to produce the same outcome as it has in the past, it is attempting to maintain its current state. It only reacts to changes to provide a previously determined outcome. The Open Organization Model can assist an organization either to maintain more effectively its current state or to design new directions and outcomes. Maintaining a current state can be effective. For example, maintaining current states that produce good results for the customer enhances revenue.

Goal Seeking. As contrasted with a state-maintaining system, goal seeking describes a system that reacts differently to an internal or external event to produce a different outcome than it has in the past. For example, the automatic pilot on an airplane seeks a given end state. Its goal is to reach a specific destination. The auto pilot chooses from various speeds and altitudes to keep the plane on course. The Open Organization Model helps organizations determine whether they should make changes to the vision, mission, goals, and purposes of subsystem functions. These elements allow a system to seek new outcomes for the organization and to modify existing processes to achieve different outcomes. The process is the epitome of human achievement.

Purposive. A purposive system can produce the same outcome in different ways or it can produce different outcomes in the same way. It can select or change goals as well as select the means to achieve those goals. A purposive system can make complex decisions and display a will. The Open Organization Model assumes that organizations are purposive, and that their members can create multiple paths to reach their goals.

Equifinality. This quality describes the ability of a system to achieve the same end using different means. In other words, there are multiple paths to reach the same end. Consequently, the Open Organization Model offers a wide range of strategies to accomplish an organization's articulated goals in an organized, process-oriented, comprehensible way.

Feedback, Feedthrough, and Feedforward Mechanisms. These qualities involve feeding information in and out of the system to produce corrective change in the total system's performance. In any system, communication and control subsystems operate to maintain a steady state or to produce a change in the system. For example, on a production line, the purpose of the quality control system is to maintain a steady state of product quality. In a management system, the purpose of the performance appraisal interview is either to maintain or to improve an employee's performance. The Open Organization Model examines the existence and health of such mechanisms in the organization: feedforward to modify constraints, feedthrough to align purpose, and feedback to improve performance and to recognize achievement.

Input-Output Analysis. This simple device explains an organization's relationship with its environment. Input-output analysis examines the flow of materials, ideas, concepts, people, money, and so on, from the beginning to the end of the system. A diagram of input-output analysis is shown in Figure A.1, which illustrates the concept of the Open Organization Model as an energy exchange system centered on all functions, but especially on people. Energy is input from the environment, a

Figure A.1. Input-Output Analysis.

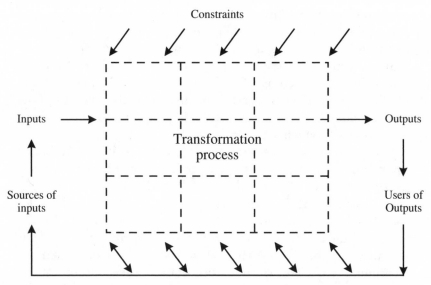

Feedback, feedthrough, and feedforward mechanisms

patterned internal activity transforms that energy into output, which in turn provokes new energy input. (The nine-box matrix in the center represents the Open Organization Model; therefore the internal bidirectional arrows of the model are implied.) The transformation occurs as modified by constraints. The organization is thus seen as an open system engaged in constant transactions with its environment, which can be visualized as a system of systems. These systems include the subsystems within the corporations (divisions, departments), which are constantly engaged in energy exchanges, and the systems operating outside, but affecting, the organization including members of the same industry, competing industries, suppliers, government institutions, and so on (Fabun, 1967, p. 12).

This input-output analysis device also lies at the heart of the single- and double-loop learning processes mentioned in Chapter Three. When feedback mechanisms inform only the transformation process (or behaviors), only single-loop learning occurs. The quality control measures on an assembly line, for instance, reflect a single-loop process. However, when feedback mechanisms also address inputs such as purpose, mission, and governing values, double-loop learning occurs. Double-loop learning, which allows an organization to challenge and abandon outdated rules and assumptions, is at the heart of process reengineering as defined by Michael Hammer and James Champy (1993). Process reengineering means radically changing how work is done; it requires the rethinking and redesigning of those processes by which work is created.

A good example of an organization exhibiting these dimensions of a system is a symphonic orchestra when it plays a complex piece of classical music. In order to perform the entire composition, the string, percussion, and horn sections depend on one another to play their parts accurately. Should the violins come in late, the orchestra's total performance is affected. And, correspondingly, when all of the sections play their instruments well, and in time with one another, the music becomes a composition — something other and larger than the separate scores. As each part of the system performs its role, it enhances the performance of the others and thus the total performance.

Summary

The Open Organization Model presented in this book is deeply rooted in systems thinking and general systems theory. It reflects the characteristics of the organismic paradigm (with some influences from the mechanistic) by focusing on wholeness of the organization — on the dimensions of unity, internal responsiveness, and external responsiveness. Shared values and purpose express the goal seeking and purposiveness of the system. Attention is on the interrelationships between subsystems (through feedback, feedthrough, and feedforward mechanisms) and on alignment to shared values and purpose. Incorporation of the external environment (among the systems external to the organization) infuses the organization with energy. The more open a system is to energy and information sources, the more capable it becomes at managing routine changes and initiating organizational transformation.

Healthy individuals, groups, and organizations may all be viewed as unified, open systems, behaving in congruence with their social values. Such self-managed people (or systems) reflect a potency and the motivation to learn and transform. A unified self-concept enhances their ability to care for, interact with, and influence others. At the same time, they will give themselves permission to take action or to protect themselves as the situation warrants. The outputs of these high-performing people will also reflect the essence of every other organizational component.

The windows of the Open Organization Model provide a framework to guide your study of and intervention in human systems and to enhance your understanding of the interrelationships present in organizational systems. Through such a model you can more clearly grasp that everything is related to everything else and that all systems can be seen within one great circumscribed whole. Human energy in terms of the modern organization's learning and transformative requirements is truly the heart of the matter.

B

TOOLS AND APPROACHES FOR INTERVENTION AT THE INDIVIDUAL, GROUP, AND ORGANIZATIONAL LEVELS

This appendix lists descriptions of widely used diagnostic tools, surveys, and instruments as well as an assortment of activities that help create and support open organizations. The matrix in Table B.1 matches each tool, survey, instrument, or activity to the windows in the model that best apply. (Refer to Figure B.1 for descriptions of each window.) A list of references that describe these interventions in greater detail appears below.

Action Learning (Action Informs Learning)

Pedler, M. (ed.). *Action Learning in Practice.* Aldershot, Hants, England: Gower, 1983, 297 pp.

Action Research (Data Informs Action)

Argyris, C. "Participatory Action Research and Action Science Compared: A Commentary." *American Behavioral Scientist,* May–June 1989, *32*(5), 612–623.

Calhoun, E. F. "Action Research: Three Approaches." *Educational Leadership,* Oct. 1993, *51*(2), 62–65.

Figure B.1. The Open Organization Model.

	Unity	Internal responsiveness	External responsiveness
Individual	1 Values	2 Congruence	3 Connection
Group	4 Shared purpose	5 Quality relationships	6 Collaboration
Organization	7 Shared vision	8 Alignment	9 Contribution

Chisholm, R. F., and Elden, M. "Features of Emerging Action Research." *Human Relations,* Feb. 1993, *46*(2), 275–298.

Kemmis, S., and McTaggart, R. (eds.). *The Action Research Planner.* (3rd ed.) Geelong, Victoria, Australia: Deakin University, 1988, 154 pp.

Mangham, I. L. "Conspiracies of Silence? Some Critical Comments on the Action Research Special Issue, February 1993." *Human Relations,* Oct. 1993, *46*(10), 1243–1251.

Action Science (Metalearning: Model II)

Argyris, C. "Participatory Action Research and Action Science Compared: A Commentary." *American Behavioral Scientist,* May–June 1989, *32*(5), 612–623.

Argyris, C. "Education for Leading-Learning." *Organizational Dynamics,* Winter 1993, *21*(3), 5–17.

Argyris, C., Putnam, R., and Smith, D. *Action Science: Concepts, Methods, and Skills for Research and Intervention.* San Francisco: Jossey-Bass, 1985, 480 pp.

Table B.1. Open Organization Intervention Matrix.

Type of Intervention	Individual			Group			Organization		
	1	2	3	4	5	6	7	8	9
Action Learning (action informs learning)	X	X	X						
Action Research (data informs action)					X	X		X	X
Action Science (meta-learning; Model II)	X	X	X	X	X	X	X	X	X
Benchmarking						X			X
Building High-Performance Climates					X			X	
Career Development	X	X	X						X
Coaching/Counseling Skills				X	X				
Conflict Management				X	X				X
Customer Surveys						X			X
Decision Making		X			X				
Employee Communications Programs					X				
Employee Satisfaction/Climate Surveys								X	
Feedback—Giving and Receiving				X	X			X	
Focus Groups						X			X
Goal/Objective Setting	X			X			X		
Group Facilitation Skills					X				
Human Resource Audit								X	X
Human Resource Planning			X		X		X		X
Leadership Training/Management Development	X			X	X		X	X	
Market Research and Analysis					X	X			X
Marketing Programs									X
Matrix Management						X		X	
Participative Management/Employee Involvement Programs					X		X	X	
Personal Development • Counseling • Psychotherapy	X	X	X						
Personal Effectiveness (time and stress management)	X	X	X						
Problem Solving		X	X		X	X		X	X
Process Consultation				X			X		
Process Improvement Techniques					X	X		X	X
Quality Circles					X	X			X
Recognizing Individual Differences			X		X				
Strategic Planning								X	X
Strategic Thinking			X			X			X
Team Building			X	X	X	X		X	
Total Quality Management							X	X	X
Vision/Mission Building	X			X			X		

Argyris, C., and Schön, D. *Theory in Practice: Increasing Professional Effectiveness.* San Francisco: Jossey-Bass, 1974, 224 pp.
Reason, P. *Human Inquiry in Action: Developments in New Paradigm Research.* Newbury Park, Calif.: Sage, 1988, 242 pp.

Benchmarking

Crespy, C. "Export Benchmarking: Export Practices Associated with Superior Performance." *Journal of Business and Industrial Marketing,* Spring 1993, *8*(1), 36–44.
Kemmerer, B. E. "The Growing Use of Benchmarking in Managing Cultural Diversity." *Business Forum,* Winter–Spring 1993, *18*(1–2), 38–40.
Spendolini, M. J. "The Benchmarking Process." *Compensation and Benefits Review,* Sept.–Oct. 1992, *24*(5), 21–28.
Vaziri, H. K. "Questions to Answer Before Benchmarking." *Planning Review,* Jan.–Feb. 1993, *21*(1), 37.

Building High-Performance Climates

Mink, O. G., Owen, K. Q., and Mink, B. P. *Developing High-Performance People: The Art of Coaching.* Reading, Mass.: Addison-Wesley, 1993, 271 pp.

Career Development

Bolles, R. N. *What Color Is Your Parachute?* Berkeley, Calif.: Ten Speed Press, 1994 (updated annually).
Stamp, G. "The Individual, the Organization and the Path to Mutual Appreciation." *Personnel Management,* July 1989, *21*(7), 28–31. (career assessment)
Wallum, P. "A Broader View of Succession Planning." *Personnel Management,* Sept. 1993, *25*(9), 42–45.
Wolfson, B. "The Human Race." *Management Today,* June 1988, p. 5. (staff development, a company's most important asset)

Coaching/Counseling Skills

Evered, R., and Selman, J. "Coaching and the Art of Management." *Organizational Dynamics,* 1989, *18*(2), 16–32.
Grensing, L. "Employee 'Personal Problems': Should You Get Involved?" *Manage,* Oct. 1988, *40*(3), 30–33.
Lorinc, J. "The Mentor Gap: Older Men Guiding Younger Women: The Perils and Payoffs." *Canadian Business,* Sept. 1990, *63*(9), 93–95.
Mink, O. G., Owen, K. Q., and Mink, B. P. *Developing High-Performance People: The Art of Coaching.* Reading, Mass.: Addison-Wesley, 1993, 271 pp.

Conflict Management

Beskerville, D. M. "How Do You Manage Conflict?" *Black Enterprise,* May 1993, *23*(10), 62–66.
Bogetoft, P. "A Note on Conflict Resolution and Truthtelling." *European Journal of Operational Research,* July 1992, *60*(1), 109–116.
Finkel, L. M. "Teaching Managers to Mediate Win-Win Solutions." *Employment Relations Today,* Spring 1991, *18*(1), 71–78.
Fisher, R., and Ury, W. *Getting to Yes: Negotiating Agreement Without Giving In.* New York: Penguin Books, 1981, 163 pp.

Customer Surveys

Brasky, J. D. "A Customer-Survey Tool: Using the 'Quality Sample.'" *Cornell Hotel and Restaurant Administration Quarterly,* Dec. 1992, *33*(6), 18–25.
Lammers, T. "The Smart Customer Survey." *Inc.,* Nov. 1992, *14*(11), 133–135.
Nadler, P. S. "Surveys Are a Popular Tool, But Beware of the Pitfalls." *American Banker,* Oct. 22, 1984, *149,* 6–7.

Decision Making

Abbasi, S. M. "Dissent: An Important But Neglected Factor in Decision Making." *Management Decision,* Annual 1991, *29*(8), 7–11.

Fiorelli, J. S. "Power in Work Groups: Team Member's Perspectives." *Human Relations,* Jan. 1988, *41*(1), 1–12.

"Group Decision Making: Approaches to Problem Solving." *Small Business Reports,* July 1988, *13*(7), 30–33.

Employee Communications Programs

Budd, J. F., Jr. "The Myth of the Communications 'Cure.'" *Public Relations Quarterly,* Summer 1992, *37*(2), 24–25.

Chandler, R. "Moving Toward Understanding." *Accountancy,* Apr. 1990, *105*(1160), 76–78. (nonverbal communication)

Gayeski, D. M. "Rewiring Corporate Communication." *Communication World,* Mar. 1992, *9*(4), 23–25.

Simons, G. "Managing Gender Differences." *Supervisory Management,* Aug. 1989, *34,* 42–45. (intergender communication in the workplace)

Employee Satisfaction/Climate Surveys

Harpaz, I. "The Importance of Work Goals: An International Perspective." *Journal of International Business Studies,* Spring 1990, *21*(1), 75–93.

Nelson, D. L. "Social Support and Newcomer Adjustment in Organizations: Attachment Theory at Work?" *Journal of Organizational Behavior,* Nov. 1991, *12*(6), 543–554.

Rain, J. S. "A Current Look at the Job Satisfaction/Life Satisfaction Relationship: Review and Future Considerations." *Human Relations,* Mar. 1991, *44*(3), 287–307.

Trimarchi, M. "For Some Workers, Pinning Down Aptitudes May Help Attitude." *Washington Post,* Mar. 17, 1991, p. L–2, col. 2.

Feedback — Giving and Receiving

Goodson, J. R. "Giving Appropriate Performance Feedback to Managers: An Empirical Test of Content and Outcomes." *Journal of Business Communication,* Fall 1992, *29*(4), 329–342.

Liden, R. C. "The Influence of Causal Feedback on Subordinate Reactions and Behavior." *Group and Organization Studies,* Sept. 1988, *13*(3), 348–373.

Mink, O. G., Mink, B. P., and Owen, K. Q. *Groups at Work.* Englewood Cliffs, N.J.: Educational Technology Publications, 1987, 279 pp.

Van Velsor, E. "How to Choose a Feedback Instrument." *Training,* Mar. 1992, *29*(3), 47–51.

Focus Groups

Fiorelli, J. S. "Power in Work Groups: Team Member's Perspectives." *Human Relations,* Jan. 1988, *41*(1), 1–12.

Pagnucco, D. J. "'Natural Group' Interviews: Alternative to Focus Groups." *Marketing News,* Aug. 29, 1988, *22*(18), 44.

Weaver, W. T. "When Discounting Gets in the Way." *Training and Development,* July 1993, *47*(7), 55–59.

Goal/Objective Setting

Collingwood, M. P. "Why Don't You Use the Research?" *Management Decision,* May 1993, *31*(3), 48–54. (use of goal theory)

Halpern, D. "A Dissenting View of MBO." *Public Personnel Management,* Fall 1990, *19*(3), 321–331.

Harpaz, I. "The Importance of Work Goals: An International Perspective." *Journal of International Business Studies,* Spring 1990, *21*(1), 75–93.

"Objective Setting and Performance Achievement." *International Journal of Bank Marketing,* May 1, 1993, *11*(2), 21–24.

Group Facilitation Skills

Kayser, T. *Mining Group Gold: How to Cash in on the Collaborative Brain Power of a Group.* El Segundo, Calif.: Serif, 1990, 178 pp.

Mink, O. G., Mink, B. P., and Owen, K. Q. *Groups at Work.* Englewood Cliffs, N.J.: Educational Technology Publications, 1987, 279 pp.

Human Resource Audit

McBrayne, I. "Audit in the Human Resources Field." *Public Administration,* Autumn 1990, *68*(3), 369–375.

Richardson, H. L. "If Only I Could Hire One More Person." *Transportation and Distribution,* Aug. 1993, *34*(8), 50.

Human Resource Planning

Schein, E. H. *Career Dynamics: Matching Individual and Organizational Needs.* Reading, Mass.: Addison-Wesley, 1987, 276 pp.

Walker, J. W. "Human Resource Roles for the 1990s." *Human Resource Planning,* Feb. 1989, *12*(1), 55–61.

Leadership Training/Management Development

Conger, J. A. "Personal Growth Training: Snake Oil or Pathway to Leadership?" *Organizational Dynamics,* Summer 1993, *22*(1), 19–30.

Conger, J. A. "The Brave New World of Leadership Training." *Organizational Dynamics,* Winter 1993, *21*(3), 46–58.

Mashaw, J. M. "Developing Your Manager's Leadership Ability." *Management Quarterly,* Summer 1992, *33*(2), 30–32.

Rothwell, S. "Human Resources Management." *Journal of General Management,* Summer 1993, *18*(4), 520–532.

Market Research and Analysis

da Costa, C. "The Key to Understanding Your Market." *Accountancy,* Oct. 1989, *104*(1154), 110–111.

Flores, F. "Innovation by Listening Carefully to Customers." *Long Range Planning,* June 1993, *26*(3), 95–102. (businesses need to be consumer oriented)

Morello, G. "The Hidden Dimensions of Marketing." *Journal of the Market Research Society,* Oct. 1993, *35*(4), 294–314.

Ohta, H. "An Information-Theoretic Approach to Consumer Preference and Product Planning." *Computers and Industrial Engineering,* Oct. 1993, *24*(3), 511–522.

Pagnucco, D. J. "'Natural Group' Interviews: Alternative to Focus Groups.'" *Marketing News,* Aug. 29, 1988, *22*(18), 44.

Marketing Programs

Graham, J. R. "Evaluating Marketing Programs." *National Underwriter Property and Casualty-Risk and Benefits Management,* Nov. 2, 1992, *96*,(44), 17, 20, 21.

Mummert, H. "Finding New Ways to Reach Your Customers." *Target Marketing,* Sept. 1993, *16*(9), 24–27.

Matrix Management

Burns, L. R. "Adoption and Abandonment of Matrix Management Programs: Effects of Organizational Characteristics and Interorganizational Networks." *Academy of Management Journal,* Feb. 1993, *26*(1), 106–138.

Dangot-Simpkin, G. "Making Matrix Management a Success." *Supervisory Management,* Nov. 1991, *36*(11), 1–2.

Fuller, L. P. "Management: Matrix for Success." *Progressive Architecture,* May 1986, *67,* 61–63.

Kolton, E. "Team Players." *Inc.,* Sept. 1984, *6,* 140–142. (matrix management system for business)

McCollum, J. K. "The Effects of Matrix Organizational Size and Number of Project Assignments on Performance." *IEEE Transactions on Engineering Management,* Feb. 1991, *38*(1), 75–78.

Welter, T. R. "How to Build and Operate a Product-Design Team." *Industry Week,* Apr. 16, 1990, *239*(8), 35–40.

Participative Management

Fischer, B. "What Are You Doing to My Job?" *Journal for Quality and Participation,* Mar. 1993, *16*(2), 46–50. (changing employee roles)

Packard, T. "Managers' and Workers' Views of the Dimensions of Participation in Organizational Decision Making." *Administration in Social Work,* Spring 1993, *17*(2), 53–65.

Pickard, J. "The Real Meaning of Empowerment." *Personnel Management,* Nov. 1993, *25*(11), 28–33.

Wallace, G. W. "Empowerment Is Work, Not Magic." *Journal for Quality and Participation,* Sept. 1993, *16*(5), 10–14.

Weber, J. "Letting Go Is Hard to Do." *Business Week,* Annual 1993, nSPEISS, 218–219.

Personal Development

- Counseling
Murray, K. "Some Employees Now Turn to a Computer for Counseling." *The Journal of Commerce and Commercial,* Oct. 5, 1992, *394*(27827), 12–A.
Sargent, A. G. "Managing Adult Transitions." *Training and Development Journal,* Dec. 1988, *42*(12), 58–60.

- Psychotherapy
Goode, E. "Getting Off the Couch for Good." *U.S. News and World Report,* Jan. 23, 1989, *106*(3), 62. (knowing when to leave psychotherapy)
Goode, E. "Does Psychotherapy Work?" *U.S. News and World Report.* May 24, 1993, *114*(20), 55–62.
Rogers, C. *On Becoming a Person: A Therapist's View of Psychotherapy.* Boston: Houghton Mifflin, 1961, 420 pp.
"Therapy for the 1990s: Quick Mental Health Treatment for People with Little Time or Money." *U.S. News and World Report,* Jan. 13, 1992, *112*(1), 55–56.

Personal Effectiveness (Time and Stress Management)

Lindberg, R. E. "Creatively Coping with Job Stress." *Association Management,* Oct. 1990, *42*(10), 80–84.
Matthews, J. "Stress Inc." *CA Magazine,* Oct. 1992, *125*(10), 34–37. (job stress)
O'Connell, S. E. "New Year's Resolution for 1992." *HR Magazine,* Jan. 1992, *37*(1), 29–30.
Rodgers, C. S. "The Flexible Workplace: What Have We Learned?" *Human Resource Management,* Fall 1992, *31*(3), 183–199. (special issue on work and family)
Slaven, G. "Time Management Training: Does It Transfer to the Workplace?" *Journal of Managerial Psychology,* Jan. 1993, *8*(1), 20–28.

Problem Solving

Fiorelli, J. S. "Power in Work Groups: Team Member's Perspectives." *Human Relations,* Jan. 1988, *41*(1), 1–12.

Process Consultation

Burke, W. W. *Organizational Development: A Normative View.* Reading, Mass.: Addison-Wesley, 1987, 189 pp.

Process Improvement Techniques

Davenport, T. "Need Radical Innovation and Continuous Improvement? Integrate Process Reengineering and TQM." *Planning Review,* May–June 1993, *21*(3), 6–12.
McCormack, S. "TQM: Getting It Right the First Time." *Training and Development,* June 1992, *46*(6), 43–46.

Quality Circles

Dewar, D. *Quality Circles: Answers to One Hundred Frequently Asked Questions.* Red Bluff, Calif.: Dewar Associates, 1979, 48 pp.
Likert, R. *New Patterns of Management.* New York: McGraw-Hill, 1961, 272 pp.
Mink, O. G., Mink, B. P., and Owen, K. Q. *Groups at Work.* Englewood Cliffs, N.J.: Educational Technology Publications, 1987, 279 pp.
Reich, R. B. "The Profession of Management." *The New Republic,* June 27, 1981, pp. 27–32.
Scholtes, P. *The Team Handbook: How to Use Teams to Improve Quality.* Madison, Wis.: Joiner Associates, 1988.

Recognizing Individual Differences

Mink, O. G., Mink, B. P., and Owen, K. Q. *Groups at Work.* Englewood Cliffs, N.J.: Educational Technology Publications, 1987, 279 pp.
Mink, O. G., Owen, K. Q., and Mink, B. P. *Developing High-Performance People: The Art of Coaching.* Reading, Mass.: Addison-Wesley, 1993, 271 pp.

Strategic Planning

Tenaglia, M. "Scenario-Based Strategic Planning: A Process for Building Top Management Consensus." *Planning Review,* Mar.-Apr. 1992, *20*(2), 12–19.
Vaziri, H. K. "Questions to Answer Before Benchmarking." *Planning Review,* Jan.–Feb. 1993, *21*(1), 37.

Strategic Thinking

Akao, Y. *Hoshin Kanri.* Portland, Ore.: Productivity Press, 1991.

Team Building

Mink, O. G., Mink, B. P., and Owen, K. Q. *Groups at Work.* Englewood Cliffs, N.J.: Educational Technology Publications, 1987, 279 pp.
Scholtes, P. *The Team Handbook: How to Use Teams to Improve Quality.* Madison, Wis.: Joiner Associates, 1988.

Total Quality Management

Davenport, T. "Need Radical Innovation and Continuous Improvement? Integrate Process Reengineering and TQM." *Planning Review,* May–June 1993, *21*(3), 6–12.
McCormack, S. "TQM: Getting It Right the First Time." *Training and Development,* June 1992, *46*(6), 43–46.

Vision/Mission Building

Mink, O. G., Mink, B. P., and Owen, K. Q. *Groups at Work.* Englewood Cliffs, N.J.: Educational Technology Publications, 1987, 279 pp.
Mink, O. G., Esterhuysen, P. W., Mink, B. P., and Owen, K. Q. *Change at Work: A Comprehensive Management Process for Transforming Organizations.* San Francisco: Jossey-Bass, 1993, 261 pp.

C

METHODS AND ACTIVITIES TO SUPPORT THE OPEN ORGANIZATION

This appendix provides brief descriptions of a variety of useful diagnostic tools, surveys, and instruments as well as an assortment of activities that help create and support open organizations. It also indicates supportive references, lists the sources for these tools, and notes where the instructions for the activities may be obtained. Most of these items are available either from Oscar Mink, c/o Organization and Human Resource Development Associates (OHRD Associates), 1208 Somerset Avenue, Austin, TX 78753, (512) 837-9371, fax (512) 835-4998; or from Barbara Mink and Keith Owen, Somerset Consulting Group, 3415 Greystone Drive, Suite 307, Austin, TX 78731, (512) 346-0076, fax (512) 346-0482. When that is not the case, the source will be indicated. Table C.1 lists each tool, survey, instrument, or activity and indicates the windows at which it best applies. (Refer to Figure C.1 for descriptions of each window.) Descriptions of each tool, survey, instrument, or activity, listed in alphabetical order, follow Table C.1.

Figure C.1. The Open Organization Model.

	Unity	Internal responsiveness	External responsiveness
Individual	1 Values	2 Congruence	3 Connection
Group	4 Shared purpose	5 Quality relationships	6 Collaboration
Organization	7 Shared vision	8 Alignment	9 Contribution

Table C.1. Tools, Instruments, and
Activities for Developing Open Organizations.

Tool/Activity	Individual			Group			Organization		
	1	2	3	4	5	6	7	8	9
A Positive Me	X				X	X			
A Toast for the Victors[a]	X					X			
Abilene Paradox	X					X			
Analysis of Skills in Groups[b]	X				X	X			
Analyzing Team Effectiveness Survey	X		X		X	X	X	X	
ANSIE (Adult Nowicki-Strickland Internal-External Scale)					X				
Award Ceremony[a]	X				X	X			
Brainstorming	X					X			
Broken Squares	X					X			
Characteristics of Open, Adaptive, and High-Performing Organizations[b]		X	X				X		
Closure Activity[a]	X				X	X			
Concerns-Based Adoption Model: Characteristics of Innovations		X	X						
Conflict Dialogue	X				X	X			
Consensus-Seeking Activities	X					X			
Contract Exercise[a]	X				X	X			

Table C.1. Tools, Instruments, and
Activities for Developing Open Organizations, Cont'd.

Tool/Activity	Individual			Group			Organization		
	1	2	3	4	5	6	7	8	9
Customer Satisfaction Survey[b]	X	X	X	X			X	X	
Designer Name Tags	X				X	X			
Diagnosing the Change Process[b]	X	X		X	X		X		X
Discoveries[a]	X				X	X			
Employee Opinion Survey[b]		X	X				X	X	
Exploring the Creative Uses of Individual Differences in Teams[b]	X				X	X			
Force Field Analysis: Analyzing a Change Effort[b]	X	X		X			X	X	X
The Free Speech Survey			X	X	X	X	X		
From Gripe to Goal in Seven Minutes[b]	X				X	X			
Game Plan Components Checklist		X	X		X	X		X	X
Group Climate Survey Technique[b]	X					X			
Group Leadership Grid	X				X	X			
Influence Strategies[b]	X			X	X	X			
Innovation Configuration Component Checklist		X	X		X	X		X	X
Leadership and Management Job Dimensions (LMJD) Survey[b]	X	X			X				
Leadership Effectiveness Inventory[b]	X			X	X				
Levels of Use		X	X						
Methods and Tactics for Implementing Change[b]	X				X				
Nominal Group	X					X			
Open Organization Profile[b]	X	X	X		X	X	X	X	
Payday	X					X			
Planning for Living[b]					X				
Power Management Profile	X				X	X			
Power Strategies Assessment[b]	X				X	X			
Prisoner's Dilemma	X				X	X			
Prouds and Sorries[b]	X			X	X	X	X	X	
Reflections[a]	X				X	X			
Self-Development Inventory for Multiple-Role Effectiveness	X				X	X			
Stages of Concern Questionnaire[b]				X	X			X	
Strategy for Forming Groups[a]	X					X			
Success Bombardment[a]					X	X			
Synectics	X				X	X			
Team Effectiveness Analysis	X				X	X		X	
Team Learning Inventory[b]	X			X	X	X		X	
Work Values Inventory[b]	X		X		X	X	X		

Source: [a]*Groups at Work* (Mink, Mink, and Owen, 1987); [b]Somerset Consulting Group.

A Positive Me

This activity is used to enhance the feeling of trust among group members. Because work groups often form to perform a specific task, the opportunity for conversation to develop alliances is often limited. This exercise provides the opportunity for team members to learn about each other without extended conversation.

Resources:
Gibb, J. R. *Trust: A New View of Personal and Organizational Development.* Los Angeles: Guild of Tutors Press, 1978.
Harvey, J. B. "Organizations as Phrog Farms." *Organizational Dynamics,* Spring 1977, *5,* 15-23.

A Toast for the Victors

This activity provides an opportunity for the team to acknowledge victory, focusing on each member's contribution to a shared achievement. It also shifts the emphasis from celebration to preparation for near- and long-range goal setting.

Abilene Paradox

In organizations situations often *appear* on the surface to be disagreements but they often are actually *undiscovered agreements.* The Abilene Paradox includes three instruments designed to analyze a group's ability to manage agreement and to honestly disclose to one another. These instruments help determine when the group is "taking a trip to Abilene" by failing to disclose information and failing to manage agreement.

Resource:
Harvey, J. B. "The Abilene Paradox: The Management of Agreement." *Organizational Dynamics,* 1974, *3,* 63-80.

Analysis of Skills in Groups

The Analysis of Skills in Groups technique provides a simple vehicle for team members to examine their own strengths and weaknesses in contributing to the group's functioning. It can also serve as a mechanism for recognizing the different roles each member plays in the group's success. This instrument, completed by individual group members, rates sixteen important process skills that contribute toward a group's success:

1. Clarity in expressing thoughts
2. Ability to listen in an alert and understanding way
3. Ability to present ideas forcefully and persuasively
4. Ability to "stay with" the topic being discussed
5. Tendency to trust others
6. Willingness to express emotions to others
7. Readiness to accept direction from others
8. Tendency to "take charge" of the group
9. Warmth or coolness of behavior toward others
10. Reactions to comments about or evaluation of behavior
11. Understanding of others' feelings
12. Understanding of own motivations
13. Tolerance for conflict and antagonism in the group
14. Tolerance for expressions of affection and warmth
15. Thinking creatively in groups
16. Tolerance of opposing opinions

Analyzing Team Effectiveness Survey (ATE)

This instrument was designed for members of intact work teams to gather information about their team's current level of effectiveness. The purpose of this survey is to take a "snapshot" of the team's developmental needs and concerns to help pinpoint areas of needed work and suggest meaningful learning interventions.

In the course of answering the survey, members of intact work groups state their thoughts and feelings about six issues:

1. The team's purpose, goals, and objectives
2. The level of trust that exists between group members
3. Whether the group is fully using individuals' talents
4. Whether group members are receiving constructive feedback from the group

5. The group's ability to solve its problems and to manage conflict
6. The group's ability to let go of the past and move forward to accomplish emerging tasks

ANSIE (Adult Nowicki-Strickland Internal-External Scale)

Psychologists have found that the degree to which we think we are responsible for our rewards and punishments plays a dramatic role in shaping our personalities, relationships, and life outcomes, including success at work. The Adult Nowicki-Strickland Internal-External Scale (ANSIE) measures how much control team members believe they have over their own lives (see Mink, Mink, and Owen, 1987, pp. 152–156).

Resource:
The Adult Nowicki-Strickland Internal-External Scale is copyrighted by Stephen Nowicki, Ph.D., and can be obtained by writing to him at the Psychology Department, Psychology Building 202, 532 Kilgo Circle, Emory University, Atlanta, Georgia, 30022.

Award Ceremony

Award Ceremony offers a humorous and creative way for the group to appraise its performance and the contributions of its members to team success or failure.

Brainstorming

Brainstorming is used to enhance the number and quality of ideas or alternatives weighed by the team as it reaches a decision. This process frees team members from the risk of negative comments and the need to justify or explain their suggestions. Brainstorming can be especially useful in problem solving when the group is generating alternative solutions for a predefined problem.

Resource:
Osborn, A. F. *Applied Imagination: Principles and Procedures of Creative Problem Solving.* New York: Charles Scribner's Sons, 1963.

Broken Squares

Broken Squares demonstrates the power of voluntarily sharing information and resources in group problem solving. Participants also gain direct experience with the ways in which competition for information and resources may interfere with the accomplishment of a team task.

Resource:
Directions for the Broken Squares exercise are from the Leader's Guide to the CRM/McGraw-Hill film, *Team Building.* The guide was prepared by Barbara Schmidt Harrison. The Broken Squares technique is originally from an article by Kenneth Benne and Paul Sheats, "Functional Roles of Group Members," *Journal of Social Issues,* Spring 1948, *4*(2), 41–49.

Concerns-Based Adoption Model: Characteristics of Innovations

This module is based on the Concerns-Based Adoption Model (CBAM) developed by the Research and Development Center for Teacher Education (R&DCTE) at the University of Texas at Austin. Innovations, by definition, may seem unlikely candidates for the label "routine." Yet some innovations in organizations are more similar to routine practices than others. As people move through the process of adopting an innovation (change), they tend to modify its components somewhat to fit their own needs. The relative nonroutineness of an innovation is significant in that the more nonroutine an innovation is, the more difficult it will be to implement.

Nonroutine innovations require more management effort in removing barriers to implementation and in handling disturbances that evolve. It is critical for decision makers to be aware of the barriers and disturbances that inhibit change, but the most useful information is the respondent's perception of the innovation. Nonroutine innovations may be the most appropriate for solving complex problems, particularly in complex organizations, but because they are more difficult to implement and are likely to be more problematic, these changes elicit different kinds of concerns than do more routine changes. This module introduces the reader to the Stages of Concern concept and provides: (1) a tool for assessing the stage of concern and (2) strategies for effective management of each stage of concern.

Characteristics of Open, Adaptive, and High-Performing Organizations

This instrument provides specific information with which organizations can assess openness and adaptability within the system. Specifically, it assists organizations in designing healthier, more open systems in the workplace and encourages norms that empower employees.

There are twenty-four items that concern the following variables: attitudes and norms related to problem solving, handling conflict, collaboration, decision making, and feedback.

Closure Activity

This activity helps give the team a sense of closure at the end of a project — successful or unsuccessful. It provides team members an opportunity to express and let go of feelings generated by their involvement in the group's work.

Conflict Dialogue

This experience gives team members an opportunity to discover and share their attitudes toward conflict and ways of dealing with it. The exercise is structured to help the individual team member to become more aware of how he or she manages conflict and to develop more trusting relationships in the team.

Resource:

Marc Robert, "Conflict Management: Dyadic Sharing." In *Annual Handbook for Group Facilitators,* John E. Jones and J. William Pfeiffer (eds.). San Diego, Calif.: University Associates, 1979.

Consensus-Seeking Activities

A number of simulations have been designed to help a group examine and improve its ability to reach adaptive consensus decisions. These simulations bring out leadership and creative problem-solving abilities of individual group members, teach team members to trust the group's decisions, and provide an objective, realistic measure of the group's effectiveness. Hurricane Disaster, Lost at Sea, Trapped Underground, and Wilderness Survival are examples of such simulations.

Resource:

Pfeiffer and Company, 8517 Production Avenue, San Diego, CA 92121-2280, (619) 578-5900, (800) 274-4434.

Contract Exercise

The Contract Exercise is designed to develop agreement and trust in one-to-one relationships within a team. This technique helps develop trust in an atmosphere that is less threatening than that created by exercises that call for personal disclosure in a whole group. Setting mutually beneficial agreements increases synergy and develops and strengthens personal relationships.

Customer Satisfaction Survey (CSS)

This survey gathers information from internal and/or external customers of an organization so that customer opinions about the quality of products and services they receive can be known both within and without the organization. It provides baseline studies of the organization's current effectiveness in meeting customer requirements, improving product and service quality, and benchmarking current practices, measuring five dimensions of service:

1. Reliability — the degree to which services or products are delivered in a dependable and accurate manner
2. Responsiveness — the extent to which providers meet customer requirements in a competent, timely manner
3. Assurance — the extent to which providers do what they say they will do
4. Empathy — the extent to which customers believe providers listen to and understand them
5. Tangible quality — the overall climate in which the product and/or service is delivered

Designer Name Tags

As individuals enter the room, have them write their names in the center of their name tags. Then, in each of the four corners of the name tag, have each person write a word or draw a picture that depicts choices made in each of four predetermined categories. Designer Name Tags is a get-acquainted exercise that promotes openness. Group members have an opportunity to meet other group members with similar interests and complementary skills.

Diagnosing the Change Process

This form provides a framework for planning a change effort. It focuses the user's attention on defining and analyzing the problem, on action planning, and key questions to answer if the change effort is to be successful.

Discoveries

Discoveries is a closure activity that focuses team members' thinking on what they learn about themselves. It increases team members' ability to be honest with themselves about what they have learned during a workshop and helps them take personal responsibility for improving their attitudes and behaviors.

Employee Opinion Survey (EOS)

This survey may be used with all employees in an organization
undergoing some type of organizational change. It helps determine and rate their attitudes and perceptions about key dimensions that are known to influence organizational performance.
        This instrument can be used to promote, encourage, and
support organizational development; employee involvement in
the change process; and continuous improvement efforts in which
data are used to diagnose needs and to serve as benchmarks
for monitoring change efforts.
        The eighteen factors assessed by the Employee Opinion
Survey can be divided into two main categories: job performance
dimensions and job characteristics dimensions. The factors are
as follows:

Job Performance Dimensions
   1. The extent to which employees are committed to the or-
       ganization
   2. The extent to which employees identify with the organi-
       zation
   3. Employees' morale or overall feelings about the organi-
       zation
   4. The norms governing interactions between people in the
       organization
   5. Employees' satisfaction with their job output

Job Characteristics Dimensions
   6. Employees' satisfaction with their jobs
   7. Employees' satisfaction with their compensation and benefits
   8. Employees' satisfaction with the design of their jobs
   9. Employees' attitudes about the work environment
  10. The clarity of organizational goals and expectations
  11. Employees' attitudes about the quality and quantity of
       supervision and organizational leadership
  12. Employees' attitudes about the organization's performance
       review and evaluation processes
  13. Employees' attitudes about career and professional growth

14. Employees' attitudes about the quality of communications
15. Employees' attitudes about serving the customer
16. Employees' feelings about the availability of needed tools and resources
17. Employees' feelings about the quality of teamwork in the organization
18. Honesty of employee responses to the survey

Exploring the Creative Uses of Individual Differences in Teams

The purpose of this workbook is to provide a type-preference profile for an entire team (knowledge of individual type preference from the Myers-Briggs type indicator is required). The booklet includes various activities that provide insight into the makeup of the team: the frequencies of four preference types on the team; effects of preferences in work situations; mutual usefulness of opposite types; and discussion questions. It can be used to better understand group dynamics as related to planning, time management, and problem solving and to assist in developing trust among team members.

Force Field Analysis: Analyzing a Change Effort

Driving and restraining forces are extremely crucial to the success or failure of organizational change efforts. This instrument helps change facilitators identify and cope with these opposing forces.

There are three values of force field analysis. First, it is open-ended about the types of individual and organizational factors that can be included as driving and restraining forces. Second, it avoids univariable analysis by using a brainstorming technique that encourages people to view their situation as a field of mutual, interacting causal factors. Third, although open-ended, it encourages movement from the theoretical to the practical, from diagnosing to selecting specific strategies and intervention tactics. It encourages clarity, specificity, and thoroughness, and it aids communication. This instrument is equally useful in diagnosing both small units and their everyday problems and large change efforts for entire organizations.

The instrument is divided into three sections: (1) identifying the change project, (2) force field analysis/change, and (3) action planning steps. It consists of a series of discussion questions that help users identify and overcome the problems presented by opposing forces.

The Free Speech Survey

Free speech in organizations is the freedom to talk openly with those above and below you in the organization and with your peers about anything (both issues and feelings) perceived to be important to the success of an individual, the group, or the organization. Everyone should feel free to discuss anything that will help get the job done, that hinders getting the job done, or that is needed (but does not currently exist) to help get the job done.

People often do not feel free to speak about job-related problems or suggestions for many reasons. This survey is designed to find out why people, at times, do not feel free to communicate with those above, below, and beside them in an organization. Some questions ask respondents to select the answer that most nearly describes their experience, and some ask for short, write-in answers. The survey is completely anonymous.

The Free Speech Survey is available from Consultants in Organization Response and Effectiveness (CORE) at 7022 E. Hacienda Reposo, Tucson, AZ 85715. Telephone (602) 721-6642; fax (602) 721-1398. The survey is copyrighted (1991) by Duane C. Tway, but it is available for noncommercial use by managers or facilitators working to improve trust in communications in organizations. Organizations and individuals may use the Free Speech Survey within their organizations but may not charge a fee for its use.

From Gripe to Goal in Seven Minutes

This exercise permits team members to share their concerns and frustrations regarding the team's work and to turn those concerns into constructive goals while eliciting help from teammates to resolve them. It is an organized alternative to gripe sessions, allowing group members to share feedback while recognizing complaints and focusing on solutions.

Game Plan Components Checklist

A game plan is an overall plan and design of intervention efforts taken to implement or to introduce an innovation. The game plan encompasses all aspects of a change effort, and lasts throughout the entire change process. This plan affects everyone involved with the innovation either directly or indirectly. In an action research-driven transformation, a game plan is subject to ongoing revision, and the total system and its various components continually adapt or reorder in relation to the change goals.

Six major clusters of interventions (game plan components), as a group, constitute an overall game plan:

1. Developing supportive organizational arrangements — Includes actions taken to establish and maintain use of an innovation (developing policies, staffing, funding, restructuring roles, and providing space, materials, and other necessary resources).
2. Training — Includes formal, structured, and/or preplanned activities to develop positive attitudes, knowledge, and skills related to the innovation.
3. Providing consultation and reinforcement — Actions taken to encourage and assist people in solving problems related to use of the innovation. These actions may be idiosyncratic, problem-specific, and targeted either toward an individual or a small group of individuals.
4. Monitoring and evaluation — Includes actions taken to gather, analyze, or report data related to change implementation and the outcomes of a change effort. These data are used to modify the intervention in process; hence, they may be used to produce continuous improvement.
5. External communication — Includes actions taken to inform and/or gain support from people outside the organization in which the change is being implemented. In a systems

environment, every influence (or force) must be considered as either driving or restraining the change effort.

6.   Dissemination — Includes actions taken to share information about and provide materials related to the innovation with the intent of encouraging others to adopt the innovation.

Game plan components provide a practical, easy-to-use framework for guiding change efforts.

Resources:

Hall, G. E., Zigarmi, P. K., and Hord, S. M. *A Taxonomy of Interventions: The Prototype and Initial Testing.* (R&D Report No. 3073.) Austin: University of Texas, Research and Development Center for Teacher Education, 1979.

Hord, S. M., Rutherford, W. L., Huling-Austin, L., and Hall, G. E. *Taking Charge of Change.* Alexandria, Va.: Association for Supervision and Curriculum Development, 1987.

Group Climate Survey Technique

The purpose of the Group Climate Survey Technique is to diagnose the "mental state" of a team and to predict its readiness to engage in meaningful, productive work. Groups in a basic assumption mental state are in a nonwork state — an inappropriate mode of functioning. Characteristics of a basic assumption mental state (from Mink, Mink, and Owen, 1987) include:

* High level of disorganization
* Low creativity
* Resistance to learning and change
* Low or poor rate of task completion
* Low productivity
* High levels of anxiety impeding change
* Lingering and unresolved discontent
* Little or no personal development
* Authority rests with leader
* Communication not sensible
* Inability of people to listen
* Increased incidence of mental rehearsal before speaking

- Prevalent negative feelings
- Low time-management quotient; team controlled by time
- Recycling of items or events
- Ongoing conflicts created by low harmony among roles
- Formation of many subgroups

The Group Climate Survey Technique is designed to help spot basic assumption mental states in operation:

- Fight/flight (avoidance-openness),
- Dependency/counterdependency (dependency-autonomy), or
- Fracturing (collusion or pairing for nonwork).

The technique is based upon the work of W. R. Bion (1961).

Group Leadership Grid

The Group Leadership Grid provides positive feedback to a team on the amount and type of leadership exerted by each member. The instrument measures and quantifies the contributions of individual group members.

Resources:
Bradford, L. P. *Making Meetings Work.* San Diego, Calif.: University Associates, 1976.
Jones, P. E. *Developing a Training Program for Effective Group Problem Solving.* Unpublished master's thesis, University of Texas at Austin, Department of Curriculum and Instruction, May 1984.
Lippitt, G. L., and Seashore, E. *Group Effectiveness.* Fairfax, Va.: Leadership Resources, 1980.
Shaw, M. *Group Dynamics.* New York: McGraw-Hill, 1971.

Influence Strategies

This instrument helps examine types of power and influence strategies, how well they are used, personal reactions to certain influence strategies, and differences between personal and professional uses of power and influence.

Influence Strategies has three sections: (1) use of influence strategies to resolve differences in individuals' personal and professional lives, (2) use and effectiveness of influence strategies, and (3) self-limitations and realism about self in the use of power and influence, personal reactions to certain strategies, and differences between personal and professional uses of power and influence. It can be used to identify current individual and organizational patterns of power and influence, to increase awareness of other influence options, and to provide assistance in designing organizational change strategies.

Innovation Configuration Component Checklist

The Innovation Configuration Component Checklist is used to identify the specific components of an innovation and their expected variations when that innovation is used.

The checklist can be organized into various formats. Two potential formats are:

1. A list or outline form:
    Component
    - Variation
    - Variation
    - Variation
2. A left-to-right format, similar to that shown in Figure C.2.

In Figure C.2, the horizontal line displays a scale for the standard developed for each configuration component. In many instances, these standards cannot be quantified where realistic subjective standards are developed and used. An Innovation Configuration Component Checklist should be developed before any attempt to install the innovation. This way, it can provide guidelines for desirable achievement and be used to measure progress at any time during implementation. In follow-up audits (ongoing action research), this checklist can be used repeatedly.

Figure C.2. Example of an Innovation
Configuration Component Checklist Left-to-Right Format.

Innovation Description

Component 1

—Variations—

1	2	3	4	5
Most				Least
Desirable				Desirable

Component 2

—Variations—

1	2	3	4	5
Most				Least
Desirable				Desirable

Component 3

—Variations—

1	2	3	4	5
Most				Least
Desirable				Desirable

Hord and others (1987) suggest developing a specific checklist for each new innovation to be introduced into the organization. Such checklists can assist change facilitators in communicating about the innovation, in determining how to implement its components and variations, and in clarifying expectations related to its use. Later, these same checklists can be used to monitor the process.

Resources:

Hall, G. E., and Loucks, S. F. "Innovation Configurations: Analyzing the Adaptations of Innovations." Paper presented at the annual meeting of the American Educational Research Association, Toronto, March 1978a.

Hall, G. E., and Loucks, S. F. *Innovation Configurations: Analyzing the Adaptations of Innovations.* (R&D Report No. 3049) Austin: University of Texas, Research and Development Center for Teacher Education, 1978b.

Hord, S. M., Rutherford, W. L., Huling-Austin, L., and Hall, G. E. *Taking Charge of Change.* Alexandria, Va.: Association for Supervision and Curriculum Development, 1987.

Leadership and Management Job Dimensions (LMJD) Survey

The purpose of this survey is to assist organizations with the development of leadership skills in managerial staff and with the selection of persons to fill leadership positions. It consists of 143 items relating to effective leadership, and it measures eighteen dimensions categorized into five broad action patterns:

1. Personal motivation
2. Interpersonal influence
3. Problem solving
4. Thinking style
5. Self-management

The results may be used to design competency-based leadership development programs, to assess abilities of individuals under consideration for key leadership positions, to select and develop future leaders and managers, and to match individual skills to job dimensions more accurately.

Leadership Effectiveness Inventory (LEI)

This instrument assesses employee perceptions of current and ideal leadership skill and facilitates the development of leadership throughout the organization. It can also be used for training needs or personal growth assessment or provide a general overview of the degree to which employees are satisfied with current supervision.

The LEI assists in obtaining the following information about dimensions of leadership behavior in the organization:

1. Providing direction—The extent to which leaders help members of the organization develop a shared sense of vision and mission.

2. Providing opportunity—The extent to which leaders provide support for individual and team accomplishments.

3. Having impact—The extent to which leaders encourage people to remain focused on the accomplishment of shared goals.

4. Building trust—The extent to which leaders create a climate in which people feel safe and behavioral agreements are kept.

5. Opening communications—The extent to which leaders foster and maintain the development of open communication channels.

6. Developing individuals—The extent to which leaders empower each individual so that he or she is able to contribute to the goals of the team and the organization.

7. Providing feedback—The skill with which leaders give and receive feedback.

8. Solving problems—The extent to which leaders model as well as encourage effective problem solving.

9. Developing team cohesion—The skill with which leaders build a climate of cooperation and group identification.

10. Achieving productivity—The extent to which leaders create a climate in which high levels of performance are expected, are achievable, and are rewarded both individually and collectively.

Levels of Use

This module is based on the Concerns-Based Adoption Model (CBAM) developed by the Research and Development Center for Teacher Education (R&DCTE) at the University of Texas at Austin. It gives the user information about common elements of the change process when dealing with key individuals and provides tools for planning and tracking progress when implementing organizational change. In addition to providing the theoretical background behind the Levels of Use concept, the module contains exercises and suggests interventions appropriate to each level. An answer key is also included.

Resources:

Hall, G. E., Loucks, S. F., Rutherford, W. L., and Newlove, B. W. "Levels of Use of the Innovation: A Framework for Analyzing Innovation Adoption." *Journal of Teacher Education,* 1975, *26*(1), 52–56.

Hall, G. E., and Loucks, S. F. "A Developmental Model for Determining Whether the Treatment Is Actually Implemented." *American Educational Research Journal,* Summer 1977, *14*(3), 263–276.

Hord, S. M., Rutherford, W. L., Huling-Austin, L., and Hall, G. E. *Taking Charge of Change.* Alexandria, Va.: Association for Supervision and Curriculum Development, 1987.

Loucks, S. F., Newlove, B. W., and Hall, G. E. *Measuring Levels of Use of the Innovation: A Manual for Trainers, Interviewers, and Raters.* Austin: University of Texas, Research and Development Center for Teacher Education, 1975.

Methods and Tactics for Implementing Change

Although arriving at a decision, plan, or innovative idea may sometimes be difficult, most people in organizations find that it is fairly readily attainable. A much harder task is the process of "selling" that decision, plan, or innovative idea to their boss, to management, or to the organization.

Researchers in organizational communication have noted that, although top management has many downward channels for communicating with and influencing employees, the reverse may not be readily available. When employees are asked to list the ways available to them for influencing their boss, management, or the organization, they initially view their techniques or resources as extremely limited. Upon further reflection, however, they often discover that many methods and tactics are open to them.

This instrument helps employees examine how they tend to confront and attempt to influence others in the organization. It also helps them identify other influence methods and tactics.

Nominal Group

The Nominal Group Technique (NGT) is a highly structured method for generating problem-solving alternatives and arriving at group decisions. By involving all group members equally, NGT usually results in more and better ideas than those produced by brainstorming.

Resources:

Delbecq, A. L., and Van de Ven, A. H. "A Group Process Model for Problem Identification and Program Planning." *Journal of Applied Behavioral Science,* 1971, *7*(4), 466–491.

Ford, D. L., and Nemiroff, P.M.F. "Applied Group Problem Solving: The Nominal Group Technique." In W. Pfeiffer, and J. E. Jones (eds.), *The 1975 Annual Handbook for Group Facilitators.* San Diego, Calif.: University Associates, 1975.

Open Organization Profile (OOP)

The purpose of the Open Organization Profile is to stimulate discussion of organizational needs and to determine what can be done to initiate improvements in organizational functioning. This instrument rates the unity, internal responsiveness, and external responsiveness at individual, group/team, and organizational levels. It may be completed by all employees of an organization or by a representative sample.

The factors assessed by the OOP, based on the nine windows of the Open Organization Model, are as follows:

1. Individual unity — The extent to which an individual identifies with organizational goals and values.
2. Individual internal responsiveness — The quality of human relationships that link the various parts of the organization.
3. Individual external responsiveness — The extent to which people in the system relate to one another in an effective manner.
4. Team unity — The extent to which teams work together to accomplish clearly defined goals.
5. Team internal responsiveness — The extent to which interpersonal relationships among team members are perceived to be effective.
6. Team external responsiveness — How well different groups work together to accomplish the organization's shared purpose.

7. Organizational unity—How well people identify with the organization's purpose and work together to achieve that purpose.
8. Internal organizational responsiveness—The degree and quality of information sharing and communication in the organization.
9. External organization responsiveness—The extent to which employees perceive the organization as aware of and responsive to customer requirements and environmental threats and opportunities.

Payday

Payday offers a creative way for team members to measure their performance in contributing to success or failure. It provides practice in giving and receiving feedback and helps in relinquishing the past.

Resource:
Burning, R. A. "Payday: A Closure Activity." In W. Pfeiffer and J. E. Jones (eds.), *The 1975 Annual Handbook for Group Facilitators.* San Diego, Calif.: University Associates, 1975.

Planning for Living

Self-awareness is basic to effective interactions with others. Planning for Living provides a unique set of tools for exploring the questions "Who am I?" "Where am I going?" and "Where am I now?"

Power Management Profile

The Power Management Profile technique is designed to assess a leader's motives and behavioral style in exercising power. It gives group members a structured mechanism for providing feedback on the group leader's use of power and control.

Resources:
Jones, P. E. *Developing a Training Program for Effective Group Problem Solving.* Unpublished master's thesis, University of Texas

at Austin, Department of Curriculum and Instruction, May 1984.

McClelland, D. C. *Power: The Inner Experience.* New York: Irvington, 1975.

Mink, O. G., and Owen, K. Q. *Connecting to Others Through Straight Talk.* Unpublished training packet, 1987. Available from: OHRD Associates, 1208 Somerset Avenue, Austin, TX 78753, (512) 837-9371, fax (512) 835-4998.

Power Strategies Assessment

The purpose of this technique is to help each team member examine uses of power. The following questions are considered: What types of power do you use? How effective is each type of power? How do others respond when you use power strategies? How do you feel when others use them?

Prisoner's Dilemma

Prisoner's Dilemma is a competitive exercise designed to explore trust between group members and to examine the effects of betrayal of trust. It also highlights the effects of interpersonal competition.

This exercise is very helpful when a group has been assigned or is considering a task involving a high degree of risk and a high need for trust. At the outset, it pinpoints those individuals in the group who have a need for an "I win, you lose" outcome. It also allows the group to process the concept of "I win, you win too" and heads off some of the disruptive aspects of competition within the team.

This exercise should not be used with a newly formed group. When the team has not had time to develop the necessary cohesion, Prisoner's Dilemma can produce a disruptive work atmosphere.

Resource:
Rappaport, A., and Chammah, A. *Prisoner's Dilemma.* Ann Arbor, Mich. Ann Arbor Paperbacks, 1970.

Prouds and Sorries

This technique is used to help team members identify their individual and collective values by listing things from their work that have made them proud or sorry. The process enables a team to then develop a list of team values.

Reflections

This activity helps the team let go of the past by reflecting on the week's successes and failures.

Self-Development Inventory for Multiple-Role Effectiveness

The Self-Development Inventory for Multiple-Role Effectiveness is designed to help team members assess themselves and give each other feedback on their effectiveness as individuals, team members, and organization members. It provides opportunities for deepening and strengthening interpersonal bonds between team members, clarifying mutual expectations, and increasing open communications.

Resources:
Haney, W. *Communication and Organizational Behavior.* Homewood, Ill.: Richard D. Irwin, 1967.
Lippitt, G. L. *Quest for Dialogue.* Washington, D.C.: Development Publications, 1966. Available from The Gordon Lippitt Foundation, 9812 Falls Rd., #114, Box 238, Potomac, MD 20854.
Lovin, B., and Cassterens, E. *Coaching, Learning, and Action.* New York: American Management Association, 1971.
Luft, J. *Of Human Interaction.* Palo Alto, Calif.: National Press Books, 1969.
This, L. *Leader Looks at Personal Communication.* Washington, D.C.: Leadership Resources, 1966.
The Self-Development Inventory for Multiple-Role Effectiveness is available from The Gordon Lippitt Foundation, 9812 Falls Rd., #114, Box 238, Potomac, MD 20859.

Stages of Concern Questionnaire (SoC)

This questionnaire, based on the Concerns-Based Adoption Model, is completed by individuals who are about to participate or are currently participating in a change process. The instrument measures people's concerns about how a change might affect them. The data generated from this questionnaire can be used to help change agents target interventions that enable the individuals affected by the proposed change to cope with their concerns in a more effective and productive manner.

The following questions are answered from the individual perspective:

Stage 0. Awareness — Is the individual concerned about or involved with the innovation (change)?

Stage 1. Information — Is the individual aware of the innovation and/or interested in learning more details about it?

Stage 2. Personal — How will the innovation affect the individual?

Stage 3. Management — How will the innovation affect the individual's efficiency, schedule, and time demands?

Stage 4. Consequences — Is the innovation relevant to the individual's performance and competence?

Stage 5. Collaboration — Is the use of the innovation coordinated among all of those in the organization who are affected by it?

Stage 6. Refocusing — What alternatives to the existing form of the innovation would the individual like to propose?

Resources:

Hall, G. E. "The Concerns-Based Approach to Facilitating Change." *Educational Horizons,* Summer 1979, *57*(4), 202–208.

Hall, G. E. "The Study of Individual Teacher and Professor Concerns About Innovations." *Journal of Teacher Education,* Spring 1976, *27*(1), 22–23.

Hall, G. E., George, A. A., and Rutherford, W. L. *Measuring Stages of Concern About the Innovation: A Manual for Use of the SoC Questionnaire* (2nd ed.). Austin: University of Texas, Research and Development Center for Teacher Education, 1979.

Hord, S. M., Rutherford, W.L., Huling-Austin, L., and Hall,
    G. E. *Taking Charge of Change*. Alexandria, Va.: Association
    for Supervision and Curriculum Development, 1987.

Strategy for Forming Groups

This exercise can be used for a variety of purposes, including
forming small groups out of larger ones, spotting individual
differences in personality or learning style, opening lines of communication within a team, and developing trusting relationships
among group members.

Success Bombardment

Success Bombardment is designed to focus the thinking of group
members on the positive side of their work lives. In most groups,
successes are not mentioned nearly as often as failures.

    This activity has many applications and is especially useful
at the beginning of a team-development effort. Not only does
it help the group develop trust and attraction, it also helps build
confidence and increases the energy level and enthusiasm of
group members.

Synectics

This is a structured method of creative problem solving. Synectics combines linear and logical analysis with fanciful imag-
ing exercises and draws on the full range of team members' mental abilities. The result is greatly enhanced creativity in searching
out courses of action as compared to the levels of creativity that
emerge with conventional methods of problem solving.

Resources:
Prince, G. M. *The Practice of Creativity: A Manual for Dynamic Group
    Problem Solving*. New York: HarperCollins, 1970.
Rose, E. *Preparing for a Synectics Meeting*. Cambridge, Mass.: Syn-
    ectics, 1975.
Kepner, C. H., and Tregoe, B. B. *The Rational Manager: Sys-
    tematic Approach to Problem Solving and Decision Making*. New
    York: McGraw-Hill, 1965.

Kepner, C. H., and Tregoe, B. B. *The New Rational Manager.* Princeton, N.J.: Princeton Research Press, 1981.

Noller, R. B. *Scratching the Surface of Creative Problem Solving: A Bird's Eye View of CPS.* Cheektowaga, N.Y.: DOK Publications, 1977.

Team Effectiveness Analysis

The Team Effectiveness Analysis technique serves as an informal "check-up" exercise for groups at work. Team members can use this vehicle to assess and discuss their feelings about clarity of team goals, levels of trust and empathy, leadership, and use of group resources.

Resources:

Lippitt, G. L. *Organizational Renewal: A Holistic Approach to Organization Development.* New York: Appleton-Century-Crofts, 1969.

The Team Effectiveness Analysis Form is available from The Gordon Lippitt Foundation, 9812 Falls Rd., #114, Box 238, Potomac, MD 20854.

Team Learning Inventory

The Team Learning Inventory was designed to assist team managers, team leaders, and those evaluating team effectiveness in assessing the extent to which a team is learning and adapting. Learning teams are open and adaptive teams — teams that are characterized by having a team vision and encouraging open dialogue and discussion, empowerment, evaluation of performance, and continuous improvement.

The Team Learning Inventory consists of fifty-five items organized into eight dimensions. Team members respond to the survey by expressing the extent to which they agree with each statement. A report that includes descriptive statistics for each item and each dimension and interpretations of high, medium, and low scores is then provided to users.

Some of the dimensions assessed with this inventory include:

- Vision—agreement about the purposes of the team
- Values—agreement about goals and objectives
- Open dialogue—agreement about the quality and quantity of dialogue
- Discussion—agreement about the manner in which the team makes decisions
- Empowerment—the level of empowerment team members feel

Work Values Inventory (WVI)

This inventory is completed by participants in an intact work team or group who are striving collectively to increase their effectiveness in working together. The instrument assesses the importance and priority ratings of typical life/work values.

The WVI is an excellent tool for promoting dialog about individual similarities and differences in core values and their implications for teamwork. It can be used for strategic planning activities in which the team desires to define its primary vision, mission, and leadership values. The WVI can also be used to understand individual differences in motivational orientation toward work.

The factors assessed by the Work Values Inventory are:

1. Individual and group *self-motivation*—The WVI helps determine to what extent an individual has a need for achievement of personal gain and power.
2. *Relationship motivation* of group members—The WVI helps indiviuals gauge the strength of their need to be liked and respected by other group members.
3. *Influence motivation* of group members—The WVI helps individuals see whether they are more likely to want to achieve personal goals through intense self-focused effort or through the use of social power to influence the actions of others toward the common good.
4. *Personal motivation* of group members—The WVI helps individuals see whether they are more concerned with security or with risk-taking and achievement.

The Work Values Inventory discusses the meanings of individuals' scores for each of the four types of motivation it measures. In reviewing these predictable and relatively stable value orientations, people sometimes find that their primary value orientation is incongruent with their behavioral style.

Other Items

The following special items are also available from Somerset Consulting Group, 3415 Greystone Drive, Suite 307, Austin, TX 78731, (512) 346-0076, fax (512) 346-0482.

An Introduction to Open Organization Systems

This workbook gives individuals hands-on experience with the material presented in the book *Developing and Managing Open Organizations* (Mink, Shultz, and Mink, 1979, 1991). It tailors and expands upon many of the issues covered in the book so that they can be presented in a training session.

The workbook covers the following consultant and change agent skills and knowledge:

1. An understanding of systems and their characteristics
2. An ability to view organizations (and society) from a systems perspective
3. A description of the differences between an open and closed organizational system
4. A description of the characteristic behaviors of individuals, groups, and organizations in an open system
5. An awareness of the amount of individual, work group, and organizational openness existing in the system
6. An awareness of open organization values and how to implement behaviors consistent with them

The workbook contains such activities as:

- Assessment questionnaires
- Values clarification exercises

- A Johari Window exercise
- An individual manager needs questionnaire
- A manager role checklist

General Organizational
Adaptive Learning Survey (GOALS)

GOALS is a software-driven survey system designed to assess organizational strengths and weaknesses. This system enables leadership to identify and understand areas that need to be changed for their organization to become more effective and efficient. GOALS provides action-oriented information about the organization's strengths and weaknesses and quantitative data that can be used to initiate change, monitor results, and adjust action plans over time.

GOALS consists of several elements. One is the GOALS Survey, which consists of a pool of items developed from the Malcom Baldrige National Quality Award criteria and from other data pertaining to organizational performance and effectiveness. Users choose a set of items that best meets their needs and have employees rate the items, using either a paper-and-pencil or a computerized version.

A second element of GOALS is the OPEN™ Software System. This system analyzes data and produces a variety of user-generated reports, which can be used to diagnose the organization's strengths and weaknesses.

A third element of GOALS is the feedback process through which employee involvement in diagnosing and prescribing system change is facilitated. The OPEN™ Software System allows employees at all levels of the organization to interact with and help interpret the meaning of survey data in terms of increasing organizational effectiveness.

Another element of GOALS is the capacity to develop internal and external benchmarks and to use these to assess progress and increase effectiveness through continuous improvement and organizational learning.

Groups at Work:
Developing the High-Performance Work Team

This 111-page training workbook supports the group development process presented in the book *Groups at Work* (Mink, Mink,
and Owen, 1987). The workbook contains eight sections:

1. Introduction to developing work groups
2. Understanding the environment
3. Developing direction (vision/mission/values)
4. Building trust
5. Accepting and using individual team member skills
6. Giving and receiving feedback
7. Solving problems
8. Letting go, moving on

     Each section includes:

*   Introduction — rationale for the learning activities
*   Learning competencies — skills the user will acquire by work-
    ing through the material
*   Key dilemmas and issues — issues and controversies in the
    topical area discussed in that section
*   Activities for learning and growth — learning activities for
    promoting personal growth and team development
*   Instruments — for diagnosing problems

Organization Performance Excellence Network (OPEN)

The Organization Performance Excellence Network (OPEN)
is a system of tools that enables an organization and its clients
to understand and perfect elements of the political, technical,
and cultural systems that are necessary to support its core mission. OPEN provides users with a network of tools that can be
used for a variety of purposes at individual, group, and organizational levels:

- Open Organization Profile (OOP)
- Employee Opinion Survey (EOS)
- Leadership Effectiveness Inventory (LEI)
- Work Values Inventory (WVI)
- Stages of Concern Questionnaire (SoC)
- Analyzing Team Effectiveness Survey (ATE)
- Customer Satisfaction Survey (CSS)

Through the use of either paper-and-pencil format or IBM-compatible software programs, users can quickly obtain data about organizational functioning. OPEN allows large numbers of individuals to respond to items that describe various dimensions of organizational functioning. The computer version analyzes these data and prepares item and dimension reports and graphs for easy interpretation. Complete guides for each survey help the user interpret findings, diagnose strengths and weaknesses, and identify potential strategies for strengthening the organization.

REFERENCES

Argyris, C. *Reasoning, Learning, and Action: Individual and Organizational.* San Francisco: Jossey-Bass, 1982.

Argyris, C. "Skilled Incompetence." *Harvard Business Review,* Sept.–Oct. 1986, *64*(5), 74–79.

Argyris, C. *Overcoming Organizational Defenses: Facilitating Organizational Learning.* Boston: Allyn & Bacon, 1990.

Argyris, C., Putnam, R., and Smith, D. *Action Science: Concepts, Methods, and Skills for Research and Intervention.* San Francisco: Jossey-Bass, 1985.

Argyris, C., and Schön, D. *Theory in Practice: Increasing Professional Effectiveness.* San Francisco: Jossey-Bass, 1974.

Argyris, C., and Schön, D. *Organizational Learning: A Theory of Action Perspective.* Reading, Mass.: Addison-Wesley, 1978.

Bennis, W. "The Four Competencies of Leadership." *Training and Development Journal,* Aug. 1984, *38*(8), 14–19.

Von Bertalanffy, L. In D. M. Jamieson, G. Chen, L. L. Schkade, and C. H. Smith (eds.), *The General Theory of Systems Applied to Management and Organizations,* Vol. 1. Seaside, Calif.: Intersystems Publications, 1980.

Bion, W. R. *Experiences in Groups and Other Papers.* London: Tavistock, 1961.

Block, P. *The Empowered Manager: Positive Political Skills at Work.* San Francisco: Jossey-Bass, 1987.

Capra, F. *The Turning Point.* New York: Bantam Books, 1982.

Capra, F., and Steindl-Rast, D. *Belonging to the Universe: Explorations on the Frontiers of Science and Spirituality.* San Francisco: HarperCollins, 1991.

Chase, P. "A Survey Feedback Approach to Organization Development." In *Proceedings of the Executive Study Conference,* Lois Crook (ed.). Princeton, N.J.: Educational Testing Service, Spring 1968.

Checkland, P. *Systems Thinking, Systems Practice.* New York: Wiley, 1981.

Covey, S. R. *The Seven Habits of Highly Effective People.* New York: Simon & Schuster, 1989.

Deming, W. E. *Out of the Crisis.* MIT Center for Advanced Engineering Study, Cambridge, Mass., 1986.

Erikson, E. H. "The Healthy Personality." *Psychological Issues,* 1959, *1,* 55–63.

Fabun, D. "The Corporation as a Creative Environment." *Kaiser Aluminum News,* 1967, *3*(2), 12.

Famighetti, R. (ed.). *World Almanac and Book of Facts 1994.* Mahwah, N.J.: HarperCollins, 1993.

Ford, R. N. "The Obstinate Employee." *Psychology Today,* 1969, *3*(6), 23–25.

Frohman, M. A., Sashkin, M., and Kavanagh, M. J. "Action-Research as Applied to Organization Development." *Organization and Administrative Sciences,* Spring/Summer 1976, *7*(1–2), 129–161.

Fromm, E. *The Art of Loving.* New York: HarperCollins, 1956.

Garfinkel, H. (1963) "A Conception of, and Experiments with, "Trust" as a Condition of Stable Concerted Actions." In O. J. Harvey (ed.), *Motivation and Social Interaction,* The Ronald Press Company, New York, 1963, pp. 187–238.

Gibb, J. R. *Trust: A New View of Personal and Organizational Development.* Los Angeles: Guild of Tutors Press, 1978.

Hall, G. E., George, A. A., and Rutherford, W. L. *Measuring Stages of Concern About the Innovation: A Manual for Use of the SoC Questionnaire.* (2nd ed.) Austin: University of Texas, Research and Development Center for Teacher Education, 1979.

Hammer, M., and Champy, J. *Reengineering the Corporation: A Manifesto for Business Revolution.* New York: Harper Business, 1993.

Hauser, D. I., Pecorella, P. A., and Wissler, A. L. *Survey-Guided Development: A Manual for Consultants.* Ann Arbor, Mich.: Organizational Development Research Program, Institute for Social Research, 1975.

Herzberg, F., Mausner, B., and Snyderman, B. B. *The Motivation to Work.* New York: Wiley, 1959.

Hord, S. M., Rutherford, W. L., Huling-Austin, L., and Hall, G. E. *Taking Charge of Change.* Alexandria, Va.: Association for Supervision and Curriculum Development, 1987.

Hutchinson, K., and McWhinney, W. *System Theories and Applications: Knowledge Area Three Study Guide.* Santa Barbara, Calif.: The Fielding Institute, 1992.

Klein, S. M., Kraut, A. I., and Wolfson, A. "Employee Reactions to Attitude Survey Feedback: Study of the Impact of Structure and Process." *Administrative Science Quarterly,* 1971, *16,* 497–514.

Kotter, J. P., and Heskett, J. L. *Corporate Culture and Performance.* New York: Free Press, 1992.

Kuhn, T. *The Structure of Scientific Revolutions.* (2nd ed.) Chicago: University of Chicago Press, 1970.

Lewin, K. "Action Research and Minority Problems." *Journal of Social Issues,* 1946, (2), 34–46.

Lewin, K. *Field Theory in Social Science: Selected Theoretical Papers.* New York: HarperCollins, 1951.

Lippitt, G. L. *Organization Renewal: A Holistic Approach to Organization Development.* (2nd ed.) Englewood Cliffs, N.J.: Prentice-Hall, 1982.

Lippitt, G., and Lippitt, R. *The Consulting Process in Action.* La Jolla, Calif.: University Associates, 1978.

MacGregor, D. *The Human Side of Enterprise.* New York: McGraw-Hill, 1960.

MacGregor, D. *The Professional Manager.* New York: McGraw-Hill, 1967.

McWhinney, W. *Of Paradigms and Systems Theories.* Santa Barbara, Calif.: Fielding Institute, 1992.

Maslow, A. H. "A Theory of Human Motivation." *Psychological Review,* 1943, *50,* 370–396.

Maslow, A. H. *The Farther Reaches of Human Nature.* New York: Viking Press, 1971.

Maslow, A. H. "A Theory of Metamotivation: The Biological Rooting of the Value-Life." *Journal of Humanistic Psychology,* 1967, *7,* 93–127.

Mezirow, J. *Transformative Dimensions of Adult Learning.* San Francisco: Jossey-Bass, 1991.

Mink, O. G. *Open Organizations and Productivity.* (Paper presented at the Valve Manufacturers Association of America, Human Resources Seminar, October 17–18, 1986, Savannah, Georgia.)

Mink, O. G., Esterhuysen, P. W., Mink, B. P., and Owen, K. Q. *Change at Work: A Comprehensive Management Process for Transforming Organizations.* San Francisco: Jossey-Bass, 1993.

Mink, O. G., Mink, B. P., and Owen, K. Q. *Groups at Work.* Englewood Cliffs, N.J.: Educational Technology Publications, 1987.

Mink, O., Shultz, J. M., and Mink, B. P. *Developing and Managing Open Organizations: A Model and Methods for Maximizing Organizational Potential.* Austin, Tex.: Somerset Consulting Group, Catapult Press, 1979/1991.

Moen, R. D., and Nolan, T. W. "Process Improvement." *Quality Progress,* Sept. 1987, pp. 62–68.

Mohrman, S. A., and Cummings, T. *Self-Designing Organizations: Learning How to Create High Performance.* Reading, Mass.: Addison-Wesley, 1989.

Morgan, G. *Images of Organization.* Newbury Park, Calif.: Sage, 1986.

Morgan, G., and Ramirez, R. "Action Learning: A Holographic Metaphor for Guiding Social Change." *Human Relations,* 1983, *37*(1), 1–28.

Pepper, S. *World Hypothesis: A Study in Evidence.* Los Angeles: University of California Press, 1942.

Piaget, J. *Logic Psychology.* New York: Basic Books, 1957.

Piaget, J. *Adaptation and Intelligence: Organic Selection and Phenology.* (S. Eames, trans.) Chicago: University of Chicago Press, 1980.

Pinchot, E., and Pinchot, G. *The End of Bureaucracy and the Rise of the Intelligent Organization.* San Francisco, Calif.: Berrett-Koehler, 1993.

Pitman, Ben. "A Systems Approach to Reviewing Completed Projects." *Journal of Systems Management,* Dec. 1991, pp. 6-8, 37-38.

Revans, R. *Developing Effective Managers.* New York: Praeger, 1971.

Rogers, C. R. *On Becoming a Person.* Boston: Houghton Mifflin, 1961.

Rogers, C. R. *Freedom to Learn.* Columbus, Ohio: Merrill, 1969.

Rogers, C. R. *Carl Rogers on Encounter Groups.* New York: HarperCollins, 1970.

Rogers, C. R. "A Therapist's View of the Good Life." In A. G. Athos and J. J. Gabarro (eds.), *Interpersonal Behavior.* Englewood Cliffs, N.J.: Prentice-Hall, 1989.

Rokeach, M. *Beliefs, Attitudes, and Values.* San Francisco: Jossey-Bass, 1968.

Sashkin, M. "True Vision in Leadership." *Training and Development Journal,* May 1986, *40*(5), 58-61.

Scott, W. R. *Organizations: Rational, Natural, and Open Systems.* (2nd ed.) Englewood Cliffs, N.J.: Prentice-Hall, 1987.

Senge, P. M. *The Fifth Discipline: The Art and Practice of the Learning Organization.* New York: Doubleday/Currency, 1990.

Sheehy, G. *Passages: Predictable Crises of Adult Life.* New York: Dutton, 1976.

Simon, S. B., Howe, L., and Kirschenbaum, H. *Values Clarification.* New York: Hart, 1972.

Sixteen Personality Factor Questionnaire, Form B, 1967. The Institute for Personality and Ability Testing, 1602-04 Coronado Dr., Champaign, IL.

Tway, D. C. *A Construct of Trust.* Doctoral dissertation, University of Texas at Austin, 1993.

Tway, D. C., and Davis, L. N. "Leadership as Trustbuilding— Communication and Trust." In the Proceedings of the Eighth Annual Texas Conference on Organizations, 1993. Lago Vista: University of Texas at Austin.

Whitehead, A. N. *Adventure of Ideas.* New York: Macmillan, 1933.

Zeithaml, V., Parasuraman, A., and Berry, L. *Delivering Quality Service.* New York: Free Press, 1990.

INDEX